D0572785

THE GREAT PYRAMID SPEAKS

THE GREAT PYRAMID SPEAKS

AN ADVENTURE IN MATHEMATICAL ARCHAEOLOGY

Joseph B. Gill

BARNES
&NOBLE
BOOKS
NEW YORK

Discovery consists of seeing what everybody has seen and thinking what nobody has thought.

Dr. Albert Szent-Gyorgyi

DEDICATION

To enlightenment and to my wife, Kay, whose intuition initiated this investigation, and whose inspiration incited the incredible results.

CONTENTS

ACKNOWLEDGMENTS

The author is grateful for the gracious cooperation of:

Dr. Ahmed El-Sawy, Director of Inspectorate
  Egyptian Antiquities Organization
  Egyptian Museum, Cairo, Egypt

Dr. Mohammed El-Saghir
  Luxor Antiquities
  Egyptian Museum, Cairo, Egypt

Dr. J. Allen Hynek, Professor of Astronomy
  Northwestern University
  Evanston, Illinois

Paul M. Routly, Head, Exploratory Development Staff
  U.S. Naval Observatory
  Washington, D.C.

Tharwatf Attiah, Student
  Cairo, Egypt, and U.S.A.

Dr. Alexander Badawy, Art Department
  University of California
  Los Angeles, California

Catherine E. Thompson Ramirez, Typist and Critic
  St. Louis, Missouri

Carolyn May White, Proofreader and Critic
  Evanston, Illinois

THE GREAT PYRAMID SPEAKS

FOREWORD

A large number of people know of the pyramids of Egypt. This groundwork of knowledge, usually initiated in school, is recalled periodically by a variety of stimuli—scenes from movies, a cigarette package, boxes of dates, museum visits, association with a fraternal organization, the reverse side of the U.S. one dollar bill, and many, many others. But besides being old, large, mysterious and the tomb of a pharaoh, a pyramid is a pyramid.

Once in a while something new stirs the old recollections, and another bit of knowledge is gained, such as that the pyramids are of different sizes and names. Perhaps one reaches the point where the largest is known as "The Great Pyramid," or the "Pyramid of Khufu," or even by the Greek name the "Pyramid of Cheops." This was my level of knowledge at the time of the autumnal equinox of 1972 when the seed for this book was planted by my wife, Kay, even though we did not realize it at the time.

Since she thought I might find it of interest, we attended a lecture on The Great Pyramid—A Prophecy in Stone. This, of course, is the theory that major historical milestones, biblical references, and certain earth-related measurements coincide in the design of the Great Pyramid. Yes, I found it interesting. I came away feeling that there was special design intent evidenced in this pyramid, but I was not sure whether we were seeing it from the designer's point of view. It was possible we were seeing it from the contemporary Christian culture point-of-view. Two things that called for further investigation were the "prophecy theory," skipping over some of the features of the Great Pyramid design, and the fact the pyramid predated this particular cultural bias.

Thinking I could perhaps prove or disprove this theory, I blithely commented to Kay that I would like to read more on the subject. One of her Christmas presents to me that year was the book *The Secrets of the Great Pyramid*, by Peter Tompkins. I read it and reread it, for it is the best overview of facts and theories in print. Then, as fast as I read one book, Kay bought me another. In addition, we visited the Field Museum of Natural History in Chicago and the Oriental Institute of the University of Chicago.

All this spare time activity, and much more, showed me one thing: Facts from a multitude of reference sources varied. To find the truth then meant only two things: try to think as the designer thought, and check to see if the results are meaningful. This, obviously, had two pitfalls, but was the only potential path to solution. First, we had to find a meaningful assumption that would prove out its validity with certainty to show how the design was patterned. Second, we had to find understandable meaning, since the possibility existed that the design could be properly interpreted, but not understood, if the designer knew more than our current level of knowledge. For example, if the pyramid spoke of anti-gravity, or levitation, we did not yet have a scientific verification check.

About the time of the summer solstice of 1974, this approach began to work out. Slowly, the pieces began to fit together and make sense—the Great Pyramid began to speak. Six months later, I had to start writing down the approach and pieces for reference continuity. One by one alternative solutions had to be originated, analyzed, checked and mostly discarded. Occasionally, further research discarded an apparently acceptable solution and the work backed off to an established point and started off again on another approach. Playing the devil's advocate was difficult and time-consuming, but necessary to eliminate preconceptions and mis-steps.

Finally, I realized I had both a subject of general interest and a need for precise detail. This duality of readership makes a single presentation most difficult. Therefore, this book became divided into two parts. Part I is the initiation or escorting the reader, as an initiate, through the lesson process. For the general interest reader, just read enough of the numbers to get each step in the train of thought. For the specific interest reader, HP-35 calculator accuracy is provided to settle the question of design by approximations or design by precise knowledge, heretofore unsuspected. Part II is the reflection or reviewing in ordinary words with the reader what the Great Pyramid said in Part I.

What the Great Pyramid says, and how, will generate quests for more and further enlightenment, and no doubt some controversy— hopefully more light than heat. I certainly did not suspect beforehand the direction of design intent discovered. I stand in awe of a designer whose knowledge was so multi-decimal precise he did not need to show tolerances, and who felt so secure in his knowledge as to joke and toy with it even in a masterpiece of communication. The learning center described in Chapter 7 is a prime example of teaching through use of a precise, three-dimensional "cross-word puzzle": This is one of the most overlooked features of the Great Pyramid!

Why should the Great Pyramid speak to you? Do you care if it speaks of pi, phi, logarithms, the speed of light or star distance, among other things? Mostly not, but a good mystery book is something else. The "finding" part patiently steps through the clues of mathematical archeology and builds a self-proving case with unmistakable precision. The "exploratory" part discusses the intriguing clues found, develops meaning for your initiation, and concludes with interpretative solution based upon the clues spoken by this pyramid.

However, do not expect to put this book down and mark this mystery as "case closed." Even though you come away from it conversant about what the Great Pyramid says by provable design intent, this is but one episode in a serialized mystery—one significant step forward to understanding both the medium and the message. Yes, the Great Pyramid has more to say, and the other pyramids may also speak, given the same chance. Then again, we may have heard testimony from the only expert witness.

Actually, working on this "case" was similar to listening to testimony from a parade of witnesses. For example, some of the "facts" given varied by as much as 30 feet. Thus, the truth of the mystery had to be deduced by overall judgment of all clues offered and credibility of the sources. No one source seemed to have all the facts, nor all with precision. On points remaining in question, I asked for additional facts for verification or clarification. So, what began as a quest, became a theory and jelled as an apparent truth, is hereby recorded and given to those who seek to know more of their heritage without mental reservation. The mystery of the Great Pyramid was not happenstance, but rather a logical plan to invite exploration.

Deep inside everyone is a secret explorer looking for "roots." Seldom is this dream or desire realized personally. Even when traces of a lost civilization or some other missing link are reported, this deep-seated need springs forth in interest and excitement. We want to be part of a discovery that changes our ideas of ancient history; we want to find evidence of human endeavor setting us apart from random chance origin or routine evolution. We may even feel a twinge of having passed this way before, and wonder where we lost the path. So, remember these things as the Great Pyramid Speaks to You; you may find the message amazing, but you are certainly going to find the fact that it can speak at all to be both interesting and exciting.

Homewood, Illinois

PART ONE

INITIATION

I. NOW HEAR THIS

Attention! This is the silent shout of the Great Pyramid of Giza. The question is why. Why should it call for attention, your attention? That is the question which led to this book.

Having established a question, what is the problem? Volumes of words have been written and expounded from lecture platforms encompassing some facts and much speculation. So, what is new? Certainly not this pyramid! After receiving some portion of the volumes of words, the recipient faces three choices, namely, ignore or forget this pyramid, remember some of the words for conversational purposes, or wonder about the relevance and significance of the information. Thus, in the third choice, the problem is located. The recipient has received a message, but what does it mean? It got attention, but how important is it? Aha, a communications problem! Perhaps a study of the medium will help to clarify the message, if there is one.

First of all, the Great Pyramid is the medium. It has been reliably reported to exist; therefore, a fact is established. Since greater credence is given to that which exists, or that which can be proven to have existed, this is a fact of importance. Those with doubts may yet make a verification trip to Egypt for their own personal confirmation.

A second fact of importance is that the medium is not new. This is a relative statement in that this pyramid is old compared to what? Essentially, it is old because the existing tattered condition of the medium displays the ravages of nature and man inflicted over a period of time. Speculation on the fact of ages varies considerably, from about 4,400 years old to 12,500 years old, depending on the

19

speculator's choice of the message to be conveyed. In other words, the reporter looks for a message that seems important in his contemporary context, then looks for a point in time to attribute the message to. However, to decode a message, one does better when reasoning along the same lines of thought as the sender or encoder of the message, rather than along contemporary lines of thought, when there appears to be a significant age differential between the two. More will be said on this point later.

A third fact of importance is that the Great Pyramid was erected. This at least relieves nature of responsibility and places the burden on intelligent planning. The medium itself tells us that great care and accuracy was exercised in both conception and implementation. If these were important, should the message be less so? No! Such an untenable position must lead to this pyramid being the result of a whim, an accident, or a random piling of stones. This does not fit the facts.

Facts four and five, location and orientation, bear out the intelligence of planning. In spite of major natural forces which over a period of time could affect the medium—such as earthquakes, continental drift, upheaval or subsidence of the area, or even shifts in the orientation of the earth—current measurement places this pyramid almost precisely centered on 30° North latitude, 30° East longitude (an arbitrary contemporary choice of scale, to be sure), with its four side base lines almost dead-on true North, East, West and South. This is NEWS indeed, due to our familiarity with the magnetic compass for finding magnetic direction, which does vary. Whatever else they may be, these two facts are attention arresters, as is the next one.

Monumental size is fact number six. True perspective of this fact is most difficult to appreciate. Perhaps someone who had dug for a foundation by hand and laid it up block by block may better understand the immense job that this medium represents. For the majority of people, the spectator type, the thought of walking up the stairs of a forty-eight story building may be more impressive. But the real question is why this size? True, a small-scale model would ask for less attention, but if bigger is better, why this particular size? Big size, big message, perhaps? Or, maybe this particular size relates to the message. Now, there is a thought to keep in mind.

If size is an important fact, what about shape as a seventh fact? Even the scars of age cannot hide the fact that this pyramid is almost perfectly level, square-based, with a certain particular slope of the sides. As with size, why this particular shape? Again, the answer must be, it was carefully planned to be what it is. Since the slope of the sides is not an even 30°, 45°, or 60°, it leads to the conclusion that the medium is of more noble purpose than say the memorial for a gigantic sand pile. Can it be that the relationship of base side length to the pyramid height is of greater importance than the slope of the sides?

The "what if's" of this medium can prove to be distracting from the message. For example: What if construction deficiences altered the planned message? What if the plastic deformation of the earth's surface under such a tremendous weight altered the construction or concept? What if none of the facts of the medium are absolutely perfect? What if we get back to the original question of attention and work from there?

So far, seven attention-attracting facts have been noted. These point to intelligent planning and also to importance. The importance may consist of a message or related messages. A communication of related knowledge would indeed be more logical in this case than a single isolated truth. Something ties what was done to why it was done through how it was done.

When something is built to last, it is done intentionally. When it does so, it pays tribute not only to the craftsmanship of the construction, but also to the wisdom of the basic concept. Consider the planning problem: Fundamental relationships are found to exist tying together different fields of knowledge; the information is universal and important; it needs to be transmitted unchanged to future generations; copying and recopying of translations compound errors; a long time span allows degradation of the medium of a single transmission; and language changes and dies.

Development and organization of knowledge is one thing; transmittal is another. Obviously, information that was important, long-lasting, and accurate required a matching transmittal medium. In addition, it required a transmittal language compatible to both the message and the medium in the same respects, and not an unsolvable riddle left for multiple speculative interpretation.

Instead of exploring all the potential mediums and languages that could have been used, concentrate your attention on what was used. This is what the Great Pyramid commands: "Do not speculate, but read me and learn what was, and is, true in a language you can understand." The place to begin, of course, is with a few of the facts; namely, the exterior facts which first attract attention.

Two questions immediately arise: Did the planning allow for the aging of the medium? What language was used? The answers to these queries are more obvious than generally thought. Perhaps the obvious is most often overlooked when complexity becomes the object of the search.

The answer to the first question is, "yes," the medium was planned and constructed to withstand the violence of both nature and man, with the latter being the more destructive of the two to date. Even defaced, the Great Pyramid demonstrates the adage, "If it is worth doing, it is worth doing well." Millions of massive stone blocks, cut so well as to fit together with uniformly paper-thin mortar joints, attest to this. Alone, however, "well done" is not an unqualified positive answer. But, the back-up contingency plan allowed for the literal defacing and old age shrinkage by having the original planned base dimensions engraved in the foundation rock surface. The incised square found at and under each corner of this pyramid exemplifies prudent planning.

Monumental size together with well-done construction detail combine both to hide by distraction and illuminate by perfection the answer to the second question concerning language. What is hidden, by being obvious, is the economy of design. The perfect combination of form and function was intentional. Instead of being just a medium containing a message, a repository of knowledge as would be a library building, behold a medium integrating the first phase of its message in its exterior dimensions and geometry. The language of perfection, universal and unchanging, is simply mathematical relationships.

How fascinating to think of such unchanging relationships being used! Even the verbal and written language of mathematics changes, just as the sounds and writing of any language change. What this means is one plus one equals two, no matter how it is written or spoken.

How ironic to think of all the people who quail at the mention of mathematics, when everyone understands the simple basics and uses them daily. However you look at it, "math" is the universal common language even to those who cannot read or write, or must gesture to communicate. Measuring by counting and comparing is so common, the mathematics of phrases heard every day is unnoticed: "how old," "how much," "what time," "twice as far," "short-changed," "what odds," "bargain," even, "play the numbers." How ironic to think the same language was used to plan the Great Pyramid.

Having been attracted to this medium, dug up some facts, knocked about a series of queries, and appraised an approach, the key must be found to verify this position. The exterior code must be cracked and checked before any transmitted knowledge may be presumed, evaluated, or judged. Yes, judged to be worth the importance of the attention it commands; and you, as an initiate, will pay.

II. WHAT IS NEWS?

Recall now from Chapter I, to decode a message, one does better when reasoning along the same lines of thought as the sender or encoder of the message. A second comment was that maybe the particular size of the pyramid relates to the message. Also, a question was asked, "Can it be that the relationship of base side length to the pyramid height is of greater importance than the slope of the sides?"

In addition to these three points, consider the effects on decoding, on not finding meaningful results, when the following assumptions are pursued. Interpretation is based on known measurement systems. The designer and builder used approximations. The design and final product did not match. These pitfalls to interpretation could lead to stray conclusions or to the perception of a puzzle without purpose.

Keeping these points and blind-spots in mind, the first step to translation is recognition of the language; in this case, mathematics. The second step to interpretation is the re-creation of the specific dialect; that is, the system of measurement the Great Pyramid represents. This contingency, foreseen by the designer, is built into this medium for those who seek understanding. Perhaps originally it was more obvious, but the back-up planning allowed for its rediscovery and confirmation.

The keystone to any system of measurement is the base to which it is taken. Without a reference base, results are meaningless except in terms of subjective judgment, which varies from one observer to the next. Even with an identified keystone, two other problems need solution to uphold it: Results need to be properly measured, and abnormal results recognized. Now comes the fun!

In 1925, the British engineer J.H. Cole completed his official survey of the Great Pyramid. Even with his minute error tolerances, which may indeed wash out in total, this report remains valid today as the most precise factual dimensional measurement of the pyramid's original base sides. The Cole figures and average base side lengths are:

West Side:	230,357 mm
North Side:	230,251 mm
East Side:	230,391 mm
South Side:	230,454 mm
Perimeter:	921,453 mm
Average Side:	230,363.25 mm

Note the fact that these dimensions show the pyramid to be almost perfect, but not quite: A planned pinch of difference to flavor the stew, but not enough to alter the recipe. This subtle hint provides the key to the original unit of measurement without distorting the primary plan. The theoretical purity and facts of reality blend in delicately fine modulation to state that the designer and builder not only knew what they were talking about, but also that eventual decoding depended on a built-in redundancy key. If, for example, the base of the pyramid had been found to be perfectly square, how would anyone eventually be able to determine the original unit of measurement required for decoding?

To say a base side represents a year is nothing new; this has been cited many times. One failing of this theory has been the attempt to relate approximate length to various ancient cubit measurement systems. Another stumbling block was the finding of the very slight differences in length of the sides and corner angles. This compounded the problem of just what kind of year might be represented: The 360-day year plus an odd amount of make-up time? The 365-day year? The natural or solar year of about 365¼ days, which would have been a good reason for four equal sides? Or, how about the more precise solar year of 365.2422 days, or the Thic year of 365.25 days, or the sidereal year of 365.2564 days? These are all fine, each in its own way, but which one and which side represents the basic annual measurement? Possibly, the pyramid represents four independent calculations of a year all averaged together? Or perhaps, none of these alternatives.

These "what ifs" just noted serve only to outline some of the complexity of the challenge. To reiterate all the trial decoding tries that ended in blind alleys will serve no direct solution either. However, to get off of dead center and move toward a solution that checked out, they were necessary. If indeed the pyramid represented the four-fold repetition of a year, then the slight skew had to be the determinant as to which one, without distorting the overall perfection. Both perfection in planning and precision in construction lead to multi-decimal conformation of correct decoding. That is one of the proofs for the validation of this decoding. Bear with the numbers as presented, for the encoder of the message was not awed by accuracy.

In order to find the Great Pyramid basic unit of measurement, one assumption had to be made so the solution would be self proving in more than one way, since one proof alone could be coincidental. Going back to the supposition of a base side representing a year, the perimeter would essentially equal a four-fold repetition. This ritual practice may be noted in the Egyptian Book of the Dead, but it does not necessarily follow that the Great Pyramid conformed to this repetition, as its construction could predate the practice. Another way around this problem is to see the perimeter as a year with the sides representing the four seasons. This, of course, would provide a long pyramid basic unit of measurement exactly four times longer than the average side unit.

Proceeding to the length-of-the-year aspect of the assumption, the seasons are related to the earth-sun relationship, or solar year, previously noted as 365.2422 days. Following through on this lead by dividing metric length by solar year days, the two potential pyramid units correspond to:

Great Pyramid Unit	Present Metric Millimeters	U.S. Inches 1893 to 6-30-59 1m = 39.37 in.	U.S. Inches As of 7-1-59 1m = .9144 yd.
Perimeter	2522.854698	99.32478947	99.32498813
Average Side	630.7136744	24.83119736	24.83124703

One of these two potential Great Pyramid units is the actual measurement unit used. At first glance the perimeter unit appears unlikely as a basic unit due to its length. If the average side unit, which is closer to some ancient units of measurement, is correct, the pyramid should confirm it. Not surprisingly, it does with an economy of design that gets two birds with one stone.

The proof of the solar year seasonal basis and the average base side unit of measurement is the slight skew determinant because the seasons are of slightly varying length. If the sides vary in the same order as the assignment of the appropriate season, the pyramid admits to the solar year seasons. Using the logical assignment of the North side for Winter, the East side for Spring, the South side for Summer, and the West side for Autumn, this order of sides and seasons is confirmed as follows:

Arrangement by Increasing Order of Size

Sides	Seasons	
North	Winter	(89.0000 days)
West	Autumn	(89.8270 days)
East	Spring	(92.7708 days)
South	Summer	(93.6444 days)

Now, if this confirmed seasonal order shows the exact side-season variances, the perimeter unit is confirmed. If not, and the skew is of lesser magnitude, the variances are meant to confirm the solar year of four-fold repetition or average side unit, rather than a side per season or perimeter unit. If not, and the skew is of greater magnitude, the variances are coincidental and the solar year assumption is dubious. The answer becomes crystal clear with this proportional comparison of variance from the average:

Season Days Divided by Solar Year Days Times Perimeter Millimeters

Actual Side, Lengths			Proportional Season Lengths		
Side	mm	Variance	Season	mm	Variance
North	230,251	112	Winter	224,534	5,829
West	230,357	6	Autumn	226,621	3,742
East	230,391	28	Spring	234,047	3,684
South	230,454	91	Summer	236,251	5,888
	921,453			921,453	

Obviously, the side-season relationship is not identical, thereby ruling out the perimeter unit, and the variation of the actual sides is less than the seasonal variation, making the average side unit the intended choice. It is rather amazing to think of planning just enough skew into the pyramid to show actual unit measurement length for proper decoding. The variance had to be sufficient to identify the solar year basis, but not seasonal basis; yet be enough more than minimal builder error and less than measurement error tolerances to prove the exact one-dimensional unit used to communicate the message of a theoretically perfect medium. What a remarkable blending of the practical and the theoretical!

Before proceeding, is there any remaining exterior physical evidence to support this unit measurement conclusion? Tentatively, the answer is yes, one. Very few of the original base casing stones from the Great Pyramid still exist, and the measurement of one is not conclusive evidence. But one reference by Peter Tompkins is interesting, even if not exact nor conclusive. Noted is the optical accuracy of a casing stone of .001 inch in 75 inches. This whole inch number exceeds three pyramid units by less than 1%.

Another approach to validation of the pyramid unit is application. If this unit is applied to the medium, is a significant message communicated? An affirmative answer confirms the unit and begins the translation of the message.

III. CONFIRMING EVIDENCE

Ascertaining the relationship of one prime dimension to a secondary dimension is the next step to decoding the message of the Great Pyramid medium. But which is the next most important? The answer is simple when two facts are recalled: The message was encoded according to a theoretically perfect medium and the medium is three dimensional. With the base as a perfect square with a side of 365.2422 units, two of the three dimensions are established. Obviously, the third dimension is height; in effect, the second number to be established. Again, the wisdom of economy of design is manifest.

Height is actually the measurement from the apex straight down to the base level, and a better term would be vertical depth. Reasons for measuring downward rather than upward will become clear after the dimension is established. It is, however, a dimension more difficult to accurately establish directly than a base side. First, it cannot be physically measured directly through a solid body of this shape. Second, as the designer foresaw, the degradations of time would diminish the actual dimension. But, just as the base dimension had a built-in redundancy contingent, so did the depth dimension. Rather than being direct as in the base, it is indirect and just as accurate: The indirect depth contingency factor is the slope of the sides.

Yes, the relationship of the base side length to the pyramid vertical depth is of greater importance than the slope of the sides. The slope is the link between these two important dimensions. In plain talk it is their ratio, one to the other. A simple central vertical cross-section sketch will suffice to save a thousand words at this point.

This shows that 182.6211 units is known, which is one half of the theoretical base side. The vertical depth, a, which is to be established

29

is a ratio of the half base side dimension and is fixed by the slope angle, A. In design, the depth was known which fixed the slope angle, A, so by working in reverse the depth could be rediscovered.

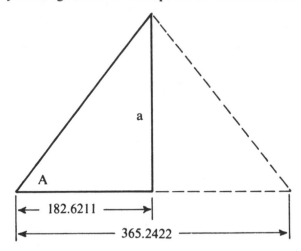

Fig. 3-1. Central Cross-Section Showing Great Pyramid Units.

To find angle A, the remaining rough sides can be surveyed or the few remaining casing stones measured. The best reported measurement of this slope angle is 51°51′14″. Digging further into the decoding will demonstrate the theoretical slope angle to have been 51°51′14.3″. This is indeed an extremely close confirmation of fact and theory.

For those who wish to practice their trigonometry:

$$\text{Tan A} = \frac{a}{182.6211}$$

or,

$$a = 182.6211 \ \text{Tan A}$$

The tangent of the theoretical angle is the ratio of the depth dimension to the one half base dimension and calculates as 1.273239545, which will prove to have significance on several points. This ratio times 182.6211 units equals 232.5204062 units for the design depth of the Great Pyramid.

To summarize the design dimensions of this pyramid in contemporary measurement standards, the following table of comparative values may be used for perspective, in lieu of a handy calculator.

Table 3-1: Comparative Design Dimensions

Measurement System	Base Side (Length)	Height (Depth)
Pyramid Units	365.2422	232.5204
Metric (mm)	230,363.25	146,653.80
U.S. Old (inch)	9069.4012	5773.7601
(feet)	755.78343	481.14667
U.S. New (inch)	9069.4193	5773.7716
(feet)	755.78494	481.14764

Returning to the 1.273239545 ratio, the statement was made that it will prove to have significance on several points. Any one of these is important, but taken all together, purpose of design is designated. This rules out random choice of the pyramid depth dimension.

Point one is that the ratio of the whole number 4 divided by pi ($\pi =$ 3.141592654) equals the exact same ratio. The pyramid was not designed by approximations! In fact, the simplest way to sketch the side slope of this pyramid is to draw a right triangle with a vertical measurement of 4 units and a base of π units. The whole number four is interesting in a multitude of relationships: four seasons; four-fold repetition; four sides of a square; four cardinal directions; four equals both $2 + 2$ and 2×2; the four ancient basic elements of air, earth, fire and water; a fourth dimension; the four horsemen of the Apocalypse; the four canopic jars; and many, many more. Pi, of course, is the basic fixed circular ratio of circumference to diameter. Of note is the use of a straight-sided medium to refer to this circular ratio.

Point two is that if a square and circle are of equal perimeter, then the area of the circle divided by the area of the square equals the exact same ratio. The purist may argue this point as being no more than a mathematically logical corollary to point one. True, but just such an assertion misses the point the designer intended: Use of this particular triangle relates a square and a circle in the classical "squaring of the circle." In effect, two simple straight line segments relate three basic geometric figures. Now the pyramid is starting to "talk" or communicate. The design goes beyond the presumed Stone Age counting on one's fingers to communicate sophisticated knowledge of the solar system and mathematics, including geometry and trigonometry.

Point three is that only by using this exact ratio will another precise mathematical relationship appear. Move down the vertical dimension from the apex to the half-way point, for example, and look at the following perfect proportions.

Table 3-2	At the Half Level:
Vertical depth down equals	$1/2$ or $(1/2)^1$ of the total depth.
Half level area equals	$1/4$ or $(1/2)^2$ of the base area.
Upper half volume equals	$1/8$ or $(1/2)^3$ of the total volume.

Amazing? Yes! Coincidence? No, not likely! By ingenious design? Yes, most probably so! Although this perfect proportionality holds true for any depth dimension (try $1/4$ depth, and find $1/16$ of base area and $1/64$ of volume), the following example was picked intentionally. The first link between the exterior dimensions of the Great Pyramid and its internal configuration is: $1/\sqrt{2}$ depth gives the $1/2$ base area level. The particular significance of the half base area level is its accessibility. According to the measurement records available, this half area is the floor level of the upper, or King's, chamber. The improper designation thus appears to be the common reference to the half "height" level.

Based on these points, the design depth and therefore the configuration of the Great Pyramid were set intentionally as just proved. So far, however, this raises more questions than have been answered. The main questions of why, or what significance, need further response. Perhaps, for example, since there are only three chamber levels (two within the pyramid itself and one beneath), each of the other horizontal levels has a significance related to vertical depth.

Indeed, the magnitude of the Great Pyramid eclipses the simplicity of its geometric language. At this point, only two straight line dimensions have been analyzed revealing a number of significant relationships. Just how simple a system this is is best shown briefly as follows:

    1 — A single straight line segment (rectilinear) provides a single dimension by its length.

    2 — Two straight lines with a common point provide an angle or ratio.

    3 — Three straight lines, with the third closing the ends of the two angle lines, provide a triangle which is special in

being the minimal number of straight lines creating a two-dimensional figure, and its included angles total only 180 degrees.

4 — Four straight lines, joined at their end points, provide a square or other quadrilateral two-dimensional figure which is the minimum figure in the whole family whose included angles total 360 degrees. The circle first comes to light here as a two-dimensional figure of an infinite number of sides and as the basic member of the single curvilinear line family of two-dimensional figures.

It would appear the designer was highly competent in the 90-degree angle, or right triangle, "game" of placing pairs of varying length lines together as a right angle, then checking the ratios for significance. Reference to this game will recur in subsequent chapters, but the two basic lengths and their ratio used to design the Great Pyramid are more noble than other combinations. Significance has been demonstrated in this chapter, particularly the relating of rectilinear to curvilinear; however, this demonstration still could be written off as chance, luck, or no more than mathematical exhibitionism. Nobility has now to be proven, and as such becomes the ultimate proof and confirmation of both the days of the solar year assumption and the first message of significance, thereby confirming this decoding approach to the challenge of the Great Pyramid.

IV. THE NOBLE RELATIONSHIP

Ascribing nobility to an angle or triangle at first sounds pompous or presumptuous; so may it be. Initiation into arcane mysteries reveals absurdity, nothingness, or grandeur depending on the viewpoint of the initiate and the method of initiation. The revelation of previously hidden knowledge is exciting if its significance is beyond initial expectations. The crux of this chapter is just that; the design of the Great Pyramid is of more noble significance than that of a noble memorial to Khufu (Cheops), who was reputedly less than beneficent.

Knowledge is a precious commodity and as such can suffer loss and degradation. Those who gain it tend to want to preserve it and bequeath it to those who follow them. And so it was by the designer of this pyramid. Perhaps a limited circle of his cohorts shared in his wisdom. Foreseeing its transmittal deterioration, he chose to commit it to this edifice, whether by royal commission or not (more likely not), so that lesser initiates would be unable to distort it beyond recognition. True, cults and rituals could preserve isolated parts, but still lose more significant concepts and relationships. By any standard, he did an excellent job, but appreciation of this fact has been limited to the stones of the medium that remained over the ages, rather than encompassing both the medium and the original message. How often this is true: The implementation eclipses its own creation!

One isolated part of the original concept and relationship that was preserved in cults and rituals is the importance of the sun. Its importance to earth and all life thereon was recognized then as it is now. This solar disc, central to the earth and its cycles, provides its own unique mathematical identification as 365.2422 days in the solar year. The importance and mathematical uniqueness of this sun number are the reasons for its use as the only assumption used in this decoding analysis (Chapter II, p. 26). As mentioned before, the designer knew the solar system well enough, and to show he knew used the precise sun number.

Another unique mathematical identification number is 3.141592654, or pi, the ratio of circular circumference to diameter. This number is a universal constant and was known precisely by the designer, even though it was subsequently lost, rediscovered approximately by the Greeks, and eventually redefined with precision. It is a fundamental number of the basic curvilinear family and relates to the solar disc (circle), planetary motion (solar system orbits), and the shape of the earth (sphere).

So far, we have an identification for the sun-earth (solar) relationship and an identification for the universal-solar relationship. Now comes the challenge to show mathematically a simple relationship to denote knowledge. One mathematical designation of knowledge or wisdom is the ability to count. Of all living things, man has the ability to count, record and judge whole numbers. He is unique; one of a kind. But in mathematical relationships unity is easily overlooked, just as counting does not really seem to start until we reach two units. In effect mankind does represent two units, male and female, or a couple, or pair, or opposites, if you like. The whole number two is also a natural number related to polarization (North and South), the diurnal cycle (day and night), opposites (hot and cold), and so forth. It also represents mankind's political divisions, such as Upper and Lower Egypt. Thus, the designer could precisely identify man's uniqueness most simply by using the mathematical identification of the whole number two relationship.

The nobility of this design may now be confirmed putting these three relationships together.

Man (Representation)   M = 2.000000000
Earth-Sun (Solar)   E = 365.2422000
Universe (Pi)   U = 3.141592654

Man and the Earth he is given to rule are related to the Universe by what? This simple equation provides the answer:

$$\frac{ME}{U} = \frac{(2)(365.2422)}{3.141592654} = 232.5204062$$

The exact design depth of the Great Pyramid!!! This indeed is a revelation and convincing evidence for use of the precise solar year assumption to identify the pyramid unit of measurement. Even if a more precise remeasurement of this pyramid should slightly alter the unit measurement, this noble relationship will not change.

Even the language of mathematics confirms the grandeur of this relationship. The number two, representing man, is called an integer, or a natural whole number. The earth number is called an aggregate, or a compound number composed of a whole number and a proper fraction. Pi, of course, is called a transcendental, or never-ending number beyond rational algebraic extraction. Linking the rational and the transcendental is the Great Pyramid depth number. If this esoteric mathematical mysticism leaves you cold, you can still shift this relationship around and marvel at three specific complex decimal numbers equaling an even quantity of two.

An interesting corollary fact of this decimal precision is the apparent lack of such in ancient Egyptian hieroglyphic notation. Positive whole numbers were symbolized, and these symbols were also used as fractions and fractional approximations. Historically, decimalization is attributed to the later Greek civilization. Thus, the ancient Egyptian lack of precise decimal notation could certainly have been the reason for the development of the alternative right triangle "game" referred to at the close of the previous chapter.

Yet another redundancy proof of the Great Pyramid's nobility of its two basic lengths is again pure mathematics. In the last chapter (p. 31), the classical "squaring of the circle" was noted. Now, if the theoretically perfect square base perimeter which equals four times the solar year days, or 1460.9688 units, is converted to the perimeter (circumference) of a circle, the radius of that circle calculates out to be exactly 232.5204062 units.

$$\text{Circumference} = 2\pi r$$

$$r = \frac{c}{2\pi} = \frac{1460.968800}{6.283185308} = 232.5204062$$

In other words, the conversion of the horizontal plane square into its horizontal plane equal perimeter circle provides a radius exactly equal to the vertical depth of this pyramid. This would tend to resolve any doubt about what circular conversion the designer had in mind, since, among others, there could have been a circle perimeter equal to the triangular cross section of the pyramid (with a radius of 152.2423399 units) or a circle circumscribing the triangular cross section (with a radius of 187.9753414 units).

Having resolved the question of what circular conversion was coded into the pyramid design, we next confront the question of intent: Should the full circle be accepted, or not, for decoding purposes? What is evidently obvious is not always so. For example, to the observer the pyramid seems to point upward, yet its height was designed to be measured as depth. The indications are the designer wanted the particular circular conversion noted, but only as a semi-circle. For example, the depth of the pyramid equals the radius, or halfway across the circle from edge to center. Likewise, the described noble relationship formula proves out to represent a semi-circle.

Noble Relationship:
$$(2)(365.2422) = (232.5204062)(\pi)$$
Pyramid Circle:
$$\text{Circumference} = 4 \text{ Base Sides} = 2\pi r$$
$$= (4)(365.2422) = (2)(\pi)(232.5204062)$$
Dividing each side of equation by 2 for a semi-circle, leaves:
$$(2)(365.2422) = (232.5204062)(\pi)$$

The architecture of the Great Pyramid itself shows no curvilinear confirmation. Nor does the interior configuration. Other than interior structural design, this pyramid is all but devoid of decoration. However, the one and only recorded decoration is curvilinear. On the upper portion of the granite beam semi-wall spanning the antechamber entrance to the Upper Chamber, is carved in relief (raised) a semi-conic section, projecting about one inch, and approximately five inches both across its flat lower edge and in height.

Speculation concerning the significance of this lone decoration has covered the spectrum of possibilities except for the designer's intention to designate the approach to correct decoding interpretation. On one hand, this feature has been taken as nothing more than a construction boss (handle) used for lifting this stone into place, with someone forgetting to cut it off afterwards; thus, no significance. On the other hand, it could be the hieroglyph ⌒, representing a loaf, now translated as the letter "t," as in tap. A more spiritual connotation of this semi-circular loaf is the bread of life. Note the word "life."

Another facet of significance will be described in a later chapter, since at this point we are getting ahead of ourselves.

As initiates walked around and around the exterior of the Great Pyramid to learn the key to decoding its message, they learned four important facts necessary to gain entry and understanding. First, of course, is the exact unit of measurement or alphabet. Second is designed redundancy to emphasize important points. For example, the same number used in different contexts such as the pyramid depth and the radius of the equal base circle. This frequency of use is used to stress a point of knowledge here rather than the common cryptological use as a word or language determinant. Third are the numeric facts established in the noble relationship as an initial vocabulary for attaining admittance and verifying interior message decoding. Fourth are relationship rules and usage, or grammar and syntax. This is more simple than it sounds. Remember that the base of the pyramid forms a square representing an area. Related to this is a radius, or half measurement (a reciprocal of 2 function). In correct decoding, it calls attention to the half base area depth as being important. So far, so good; whither now?

V. IT SHALL BE OPENED UNTO YOU

Random searching of the acres of original surface of the Great Pyramid would inevitably fail the initiate in finding access to the indicated further knowledge. Eventually, this failure would weed out those easily discouraged and encourage those of greater desire to repair to a rational approach. Repeated reflection on the initial facts had to locate the access precisely, or the pyramid was a monstrous joke—an unrequited promise. Pondering this puzzle and repeatedly plodding around the pyramid, the determined initiate came to the realization that the answer was there; but the big question was, which answer? Let us proceed to the correct one.

Around and around, the precise solar year repeated four times, again and again; precise solar year—solar—sun—the sun is a star; entrance—the entrance has to be in a fixed position; fixed star, fixed entrance: That is it! The fixed star. Of course, the North pole star. The sun traverses three sides of the pyramid, but the pole star remains fixed on one side only. So, the initiate has narrowed the search down to one side—the North side; but where, precisely? There is that word again, precise, as in precise solar year.

Now, back and forth along the North side, looking down and finding no clue, looking up and seeing nothing obvious. But wait, go back to the corner, and walk along looking up again. Notice what the side is appearing to do; progressively lengthening to the midpoint then progressively shortening. Precise solar year, each step a day, the days lengthening and shortening, but the first choice of the center line yields no entrance. There has to be something more to the precise solar year directions for opening this container to extract the contents of further knowledge. What is there in the calendar near the longest day in the year that is of solar importance?

Actually, the longest day of the year may be recalled as a truth in average. The earliest sunrise is offset to one side and the latest sunset is offset to the other due to the complexities of the earth's orbit, or year, around the sun. One must precisely know of and understand the effects of these complexities, so that the one most important facet thereof will locate the entrance. At this point we will short-cut directly to the span of days of latest sunset, measured to the nearest rounded minute. This occurs for almost a dozen days after the longest day. Thus, the entrance location is narrowed to two choices, either a short dozen days East or West of the North side center-line. Exactly where we still do not know, but the designer knew precisely, so a return to reasoning along the same lines of thought is necessary.

Visualize the face of the North side as a rectangular coordinate graph with the pyramid center line as the vertical axis and the base line as the horizontal axis. Having a one-dimensional annual unit plus an offset dimension posed a problem of how to use these on the two-dimensional graph to locate the entrance. Now try starting at the Northwest corner of the pyramid and walk East along the North side, or on the graph paper start on the right and move horizontally left. Incidentally, this is a clockwise motion. At the center is the longest day of the year; then continue for the distance of the latest sunset offset and stop. How far up is the entrance? Suppose the two precise measurements are divided, the year by the offset, with the quotient used for the vertical (or, in actuality, the measurement up the slant face) dimension. The center of the entrance in pyramid units is found at:

$$\frac{365.2422}{11.55901825} = 31.59802953 \text{ units up the pyramid face}$$

Translated to contemporary units of measurement, using the average inch conversion of 1 unit equals 24.8312 inches,

Measurement	Average U.S.	Millimeters
Offset (E. of cL)	23 ft. 11 1/32 in.	7,290.43
Slant Height	65 ft. 4 5/8 in.	19,929.31

The rationale for this method of location is simple. Looking at the graph, the offset and height measurements form a rectangle. When the two dimensions are multiplied, the product repeats the precise number of days in the year, or a compacting of a large one-dimensional measurement into a smaller two-dimensional measurement of equal magnitude. Here again, designed redundancy is used for emphasis of the 365.2422 number. This is also another proof for the basic decoding assumption of the use of the precise solar year as the theoretically perfect Great Pyramid base side dimension.

Before climbing the North face of the pyramid to confirm the calculated entrance location, another observation is in order. The rectangular coordinate language of mathematics bears a striking similarity to the ancient Egyptian written hieroglyphic language which could be written horizontally or vertically and either left-to-right or right-to-left, with the individual glyphs facing toward the correct starting point. At this juncture, the question of primogeniture can only degenerate into the familiar chicken or egg argument.

At the entrance location, a true vertical height of 24.84992591 units (51 ft. 5 1/16 in. or 15,673.19 mm), an entry door was found by the initiate. Its surface measurements were 1.648721271 units wide (40 15/16 in. or 1,039.87 mm) by 1.946800972 units high (48 11/32 in. or 1,227.87 mm). In 24 B.C. Strabo described it in un-tomblike terms as a hinged stone door which could be raised. This has been taken to be similar to an upper pivoted door found at Dashur.

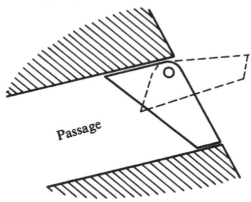

Fig. 5-1. Accepted Upper Pivoted Entrance Door

This may be a correct interpretation; however, it presents two problems: Initial entry space clearance would be only about one half of the passage height, and the door would be a difficult-to-handle, self-closing type, rather than counter-balanced. For reasons that become clear further along, the likely alternative upper pivoted door found would be a full aperture, counter-balanced type.

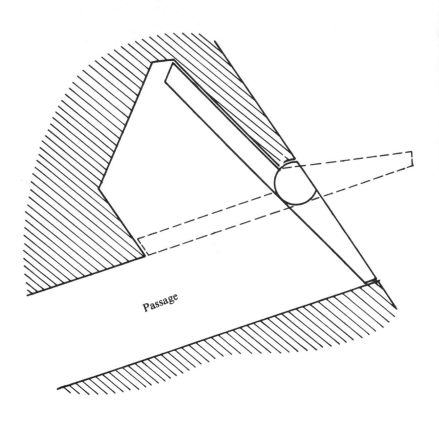

Fig. 5-2. Alternative Upper Pivoted Entrance Door

With the entire polished limestone casing, including the door, being stripped from the Great Pyramid 600 to 700 years ago, the counter-balanced door is speculative except for four pieces of evidence. First, the accepted pivoted door would have to have been rounded along the upper edge, which in the right lighting, would have been obvious as a shadowed recess. Second, the counter-balance chamber would account for the present complete absence of interior filler stone blocks directly over the entry area. Third, crawling through a restricted entryway with a stone door banging against head or feet does not make sense, particularly when a sustainable shaded, full aperture can be shown as useful. Fourth, the counter-balanced door accounts for one useful purpose for the ventilation shafts found in this pyramid, and that is to prevent air or wind pressure changes from moving the door. Incidentally, a tomb does not need ventilation, but a pyramid built for use would (for fresh air), for maintenance of a standard constant temperature (68° F. or 20°C. in this case), and would require opposing shaft apertures approximately the same elevation for countering wind direction.

Before opening the door, the observant initiate will notice something else that verifies the entry location: Another redundancy clue from the noble relationship. Look at this sketch with the accepted lintel and door jamb on the left and the alternative counter-balanced door and jambs on the right:

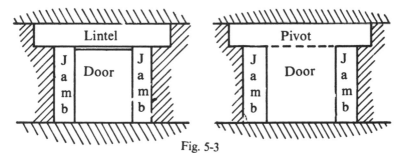

Fig. 5-3

In the counter-balanced, one-piece pivot and door, the dotted line represents a probable inscribed line. Either case then upon close inspection shows what became the Greek letter pi. Coincidence? Perhaps not, for in the Far East, the Orientals used the same basic figure in front of their temples and called it the "Gateway to Heaven." Along this same line from the ancient Orient are also found circular discs with round center holes. Pi (pronounced "bee") represented earth in the center as the hole and the outside as heaven.

Returning to the Great Pyramid entrance from this brief excursion to the Orient, we look again at the entry door dimensions in light of the method of finding it. If the external width and height of the door are multiplied, the number 3.209732173 is obtained, or slightly more than pi. Now open the door and measure the actual height of the passage as 1.905472265 units (47 5/16 in. or 1201.81 mm). The width multiplied by the actual height produces the product 3.141592654, or the magnitude of pi in the two-dimensional condensed form.

Here again is design by specific intent; precision of message, design, execution and logic for decoding. The exterior code indeed carries over the threshold to the interior where further revelations are indicated. So now, follow the initiate over the brink and plunge into the darkness of the descending "pi" passage, being careful to leave the door open.

VI. PASSAGE TO FURTHER ENLIGHTENMENT

As the initiate follows the passage downward into the pyramid alert for any sign of access to the promised half area level of knowledge, the passage changes from within the medium to the bedrock beneath. Shortly thereafter it descends past the ground level and continues perfectly straight, still with pi dimensions. Obviously, this is no maze designed to confound those who would seek its message.

After a long descent the passage changes character by abruptly becoming horizontal, past the center of the pyramid, to suddenly open into a roughly rectangular chamber. Strange, for the encoded design parts of the medium are precisely finished. Perhaps this underground chamber is not intended to be read out. A blind passage in the South wall across from the entry passage and a square well-like hole in the center of the unfinished floor denote nothing, either, unless this chamber represents a rough approximation of something surmised, but unknown, to the designer.

This chamber South of the center cross-section of the pyramid is almost as nebulous as the origin of the earth in which it is hewn, or as the origin of man. In fact, it would almost seem to be upside down, since the ceiling is far more smoothly finished than the floor, which was never leveled or finished at all. The puzzle now is where did the known change into the unknown. It is time to climb up out of this underground chamber into the entry passage and take another look.

The short horizontal passage has an irregular recess hollowed out of the West wall toward the perpendicular center-line of the pyramid, but not to it, and no sign of an ascending outlet. Irregular recess, roughed-out chamber, a short horizontal passage cutting off the known descending pi passage.... Say, wait a minute, cutting off the descending passage has to indicate the design limit of the third dimension of the known descending passage. Back to the cutoff junction and a surprise, if the initiate lives in the proper era.

Looking up the descending pi passage, as one would look up from the bottom of a deep well (even during the day), and in the very small section of sky observed, a star may be seen. In this case, however, it is a particular star, for this passage points to the North Celestial Pole star. Due to precession, the slow small circle the earth's north pole describes, and nutation, the earth's faster, smaller spiral wobble along the circle of precession, this fixed pointer passage must be used at exactly the right span of years to center upon the pole star. In ancient time it pointed to alpha Draconis (Thuban), and now it almost pin-points alpha Ursae Minoris (Polaris). Strangely enough, no others so closely touch the 25,800-year circle of precession.

For now, the reverie about this remarkable 24-hour lensless telescope must be put aside and the decoding of the Great Pyramid pursued. Careful measurement of this pi passage length provides the number of units cut off at 172.1865092 (356.3 ft. or 108.6 meters) for the theoretically perfect pyramid design. Nothing is obvious yet, so there has to be more to be discovered first.

The horizontal cutoff passage of smaller width and height dimensions adds no new information except that its floor length to the centerline of the pyramid is 9.367744000 units (19.4 ft. or 5.9 meters), and it is 52.25776870 units (108.1 ft. or 33.0 meters) below ground level. Since the depth of the pyramid from apex to ground level is part of the noble relationship, the added pit passage depth needs to be compared to it. Dividing the combined depths by the noble depth provides a ratio of 1.224744871, or the exact square root of one and a half. Apparently, 1.5 is a number of significance which the designer could only show by mathematical use of the number 2, another number of the noble relationship. At this point, the cutoff assumption is upheld, but a more interesting reason will soon be found.

Before the initiate retires to the recess or pit to piece his facts together, one more measurement needs to be taken and checked mathematically. The slope of the descending pi passage was designed to be 26.31904020° (26° 19′ 8.5″). This either had to be, or will be, the pole star this fixed pointer was intended to identify. Since this is one use for this numeric value, the design redundancy principle indicates the presence of at least one more use of this relationship.

After long reflection on the facts and contemplation of the

designer's line of thought, the light of truth begins to glow and the confirmation of decoding continues. First, the designer theoretically used the cross-section of the earth as a circle with this fixed marker at 30° North latitude. However, since the cross-section is in reality slightly elipsoidal, The Great Pyramid is placed at 29° 58′ 51″ North latitude to maintain the true 30° relationship because the actual shape of the earth was then known.

Next, a fixed star position was known, so the descending pi passage was designed to point to this fact. It tells us to look at the stars that cross its center-line and learn what the designer knew. This accounts for the slope of this passage, but what about its exact length and position related to the geometry of the Great Pyramid? Again, the ingenuity of design redundancy lights the path of one step, or fact, at a time toward further knowledge.

The key to attaining the next step is the ground level. Visualize the triangle formed looking West through the North half of the pyramid. Note where the floor-line of the descending passage crosses the base line of the triangle. This point is 115.0149024 units (238.0 ft. or 72.5 meters) to the right (North) of the vertical centerline of the pyramid. From this point a straight line drawn perpendicular to the passage floor line goes directly to the apex.

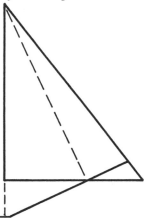

Fig. 6-1. Geometry of Descending Passage Floor Line to Pyramid Shape.

Even this conjunction of correct passage slope and right angle could be open to debate were it not for another fact introduced by this particular combination; one outside of the noble relationship, but related to it. The designer wanted to fix the length of the descending pi passage in stone which the floor represents. Once that was done, the initiate's attention had to be raised to the mid-air centerline or beam of star light which crosses the ground-level base line 112.8660468 units (233.5 ft. or 71.2 meters) to the right (North) of the vertical centerline of the pyramid. Another meaningless number, until the half pyramid base line is divided by it, to introduce the new fact called the phi (ϕ) proportion.

$$\frac{182.6211000}{112.8660468} \quad = \quad 1.618033989 \quad = \quad \phi$$

This well known ratio is significant on several points worthy of reiteration because they bear differing names.

1. The Arts—Phi is known as the "Golden Sector" or perfect proportionality.
2. Natural Sciences—Phi is known as the "Fibonacci Numbers," or 1, 1, 2, 3, 5, 8, 13, 21,... where each number following the first 1 consists of the sum of the two previous numbers, and the ratio between any two successive larger Fibonacci numbers approaches ϕ.
3. Mathematics—Phi is known in several guises:
   a. As mentioned at the end of Chapter III, the right triangle "game" would use a one-unit line and a two-unit line for a phi component values triangle, or a one-unit line and a phi component values triangle, or a one-unit line and a phi-unit line for a phi tangent triangle.
   b. For those fascinated by "games" of numerical metamorphosis,

$$\phi \;=\; 1.618033989 \;=\; \frac{1+\sqrt{5}}{2} \;=\; \frac{3+\sqrt{5}}{1+\sqrt{5}}$$

$$1/\phi \;=\; 0.618033989 \;=\; \phi-1 \;=\; \frac{2}{1+\sqrt{5}}$$

$$\phi^2 \;=\; 2.618033989 \;=\; \phi+1 \;=\; \frac{3+\sqrt{5}}{2}$$

c. For finding any Fibonacci number or to calculate the series of numbers in this pattern of nature, use:
$\frac{\phi^n}{\sqrt{5}}$ rounded to the nearest whole number, with the power "n" being the position in the series.

d. As the ratio basis of the progressive digital series (noted in 2. above) in a binary mode (basis for current computer technology):
Let A = O = Off and B = 1 = On, then

n	Binary	$F_n^\#$	$\Sigma F^\# = F_{n+2} - 1$
0	A	0	0
1	B	1	1
2	A + B	1	2
3	− A + B + [A + B]	2	4
4	− A − B + [A + B] + [− A + B + (A + B)]	3	7

These examples will suffice to show the kindredship between phi and 2 from the noble relationship. Phi can thus be read as a natural order of things on earth including man, represented by 2 in its makeup.

With phi now introduced by the centerline of the descending passage, it or a variant thereof may be expected to recur as decoding progresses. For example, if the pit passage is no more than a cutoff for the pyramid depth and descending passage length, it would be reasonable to proportion it in design with the North part times the phi ratio to equal the total length or 15.15732819 units (31.4 ft. or 9.6 meters). However, the pit terminus of this passage actually shows a phi ratio derivative length of 11.57916838 units (24.0 ft. or 7.3 meters), which is equal to the square root of five minus one, or two divided by phi. Why? It would seem the designer wanted to introduce the perfect proportion, but steer the initiate quickly to the related ratio of 1.236067977, as now becomes apparent.

Suppose the descending pi passage were indeed cut off. How much and where to look for it would answer this supposition, if verifiable. By association, the longer part of the pit passage, or North proportion, touches the descending pi passage. The missing pi passage could then be shorter than the known descending pi passage, so try dividing it by the just-found phi-related ratio, and the missing pi passage portion would have to be 139.3018122 units (288.3 ft. or 87.9 meters) in length. Where to look comes to mind when, at the bottom of the descending pi passage looking upward, the initiate recalls the promise of the half area level: Why of course, check the missing length for use as an ascending pi passage at the same slope.

In computational verification of this supposition, the initiate soon finds it may be true, if the floor of the ascending pi passage crosses the vertical centerline of the pyramid at 1.470887340 units (36 17/32 in. or 927.71 mm) below the half area level. This will be so verified when the initiate does arrive at the Great Step, as it is now named. Using this assumption does point to checking the ceiling of the descending pi passage starting at 43.33581252 units (89.7 ft. or 27.3 meters) in from the entrance.

Originally, the initiate would have found the confirming joints in the ceiling where the computation so indicated. However, the sealing ceiling block would give no sign of movement for access to the ascending pi passage. Today, with the prismatically shaped sealing block missing, the lower end of this passage is openly defined. Also revealed is the bottom of the lowest granite plug block in the ascending pi passage; a very good reason for the ceiling block to have been fixed in place.

A line drawing of what has now been located is in order to summarize design intent. The total pi passage length of 311.4883214 units (644.6 ft. or 196.5 meters) is proportionally divided between descending and ascending parts. The reason for this, getting to a higher level than designed into any other pyramid, is part of the message decoded in the next chapter. Of interest here, the two pi passage parts form the lower-case Greek letter lambda (λ), rotated 90 degrees clockwise: Today, one use for this character is to represent the wavelength of light.

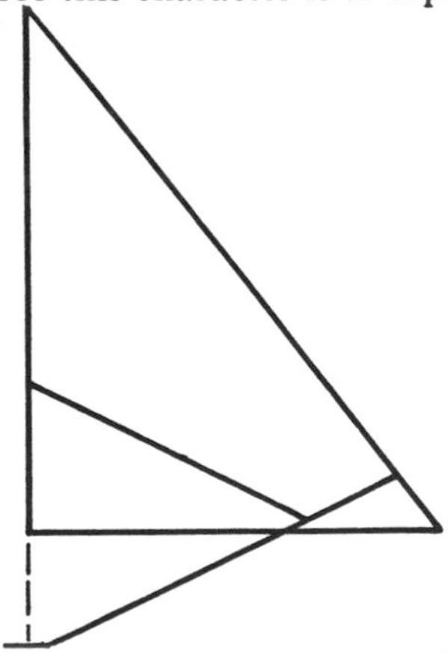

Fig. 6-2. Geometry of Descending and Ascending Floor Lines to Pyramid Shape.

Faced with this confirming evidence of the ascending passage, but frustrated in direct verification, the initiate has the opportunity to again exercise the power of observation. Clever clues do make the solving of a mystery possible and more interesting. Since reason does not provide direct access to the answer, some other token or clue must be given and is yet to be recognized as such.

With the descending pi passage offset to the East of the center of this pyramid, the West side wall is a choice candidate for further study. Starting at the upper end and working downward, each joint of the side wall blocks within the pyramid body is checked. These joints are mostly perpendicular to the ground level and reveal nothing. Even though part way down a double-scored line perpendicular to the floor-line is found, close inspection finds the pair to be inscribed lines, or false joints. Yes, they could have indicated a door, but did not. With this potential clue eliminated, the initiate continues the downward study. Shortly after passing the junction of the pi passages, the descending passage enters the bedrock with a couple of natural fissures, but no joints. At last, about 90% of the way down to the pit passage the anticipated door joints are found, and the door opened.

Unlike the finished designed passage, this opening reveals an unfinished short horizontal tunnel which abruptly changes direction to angle upward. After an arduous ascent, what is now known as the Grotto is attained. This "cave," where bedrock knoll and interior pyramid construction join, does have a point of interest. Balanced over the edge of a deep-dish depression in the limestone bedrock is a large rectangular block of drilled granite, large enough to have had to be initially incarcerated herein; designed in, but not of, the basic design.

Returning to the upward tunnel, the climb continues up the vertical, now roughly block-sided tunnel known as the "well shaft" to a jog Eastward. With the original covering blocks displaced, the tunnel shaft merges with the calculated ascending pi passage at a distinctive juncture: To the left is the confirming plugged pi passage sloping up to this point, and on the right horizontally is another passage, with the bottom half of the ascending pi passage imbedded in the floor of the Grand Gallery continuing its same upward slope above this unpredicted horizontal passage.

Before pursuing the decoding objective, a couple of reflective thoughts intercede. The designed pi passage slopes were identical, so the few modern references to the descending angle being very slightly steeper and ascending less steeply could infer a very slight tilt or pitch of the Great Pyramid plateau plane since original construction commenced, possibly a non-uniform tilt. Also, several designed, identified numeric statements have yet to be meaningfully read out against redundancy evidence. The pit chamber, tunnel, Grotto and well-shaft are of non-readout design akin to the service areas of a contemporary edifice; for example, respectively, the power plant area, the utility or service tunnel, the workshop or test laboratory, and the utility or service shaft.

VII. THE LEARNING CENTER

At this juncture, where the ascending pi passage enlarges its upper half to continue as the Grand Gallery, the now missing ascending passage floor blocks were removable. With these blocks displaced, revealing the horizontal passage to the Queen's Chamber, the initiate finds a place to pause for orientation. This horizontal passage floor reveals this place as related to, but not part of, the message encoded in the design. The block detention lip interrupts the junction of level floor with the ascending floor.

Calculation of the theoretical floor junction line reveals a trio of interesting facts. First, it bisects the ascending floor distance from the floor of the descending passage to the base of the Great Step. Second, this halving of the total ascending floor distance places the entry floor level into the Queen's Chamber passage at 35.75170459 units (73 ft. 11 3/4 in. or 22,549.09 mm) above ground level. And third, this junction line is 62.43083346 units (129 ft. 2 1/4 in. or 39,375.98 mm) North of the East-West centerline of the Great Pyramid.

With these facts established, the initiate may now focus his attention on the passage itself. Its width is the same as the pi passages (1.648721271 units), but its height is only 1.819591979 units (45 3/16 in. or 1147.64 mm). The width times the height equals 3, even. So, instead of a "pi" passage, the initial Queen's Chamber passage is a "three" passage in magnitude. A good surmise at this point would be that this place leads to an instructional or clarification phase for proper decoding.

To follow this design digression, return to the theoretical floor junction line. Here, from the known half point of the total ascending distance, follow the "three" passage horizontal digression for 50 units

53

(103 ft. 5 9/16 in. or 31,535.68 mm). At this 50-unit point, watch your step, because the passage floor drops vertically .9097959894 units (22 19/32″ or 573.82 mm). This discontinuity serves several purposes:

1. It represents the second verification of design digression; the first being the block detention lip.
2. It states emphatically that this digression is not part of the basic Great Pyramid design. That is, do not relate this part to the depth within the pyramid, because this floor line system of measurement is broken before it reaches the East-West centerline.
3. Its 50-unit length not only serves as a reminder of the ascending passage's 50% relationship, but, as will be discovered, a basis for the Queen's Chamber design.
4. Its drop changes the final Queen's Chamber passage height to 2.729387968 units (67 49/64 in. or 1721.46 mm), which multiplied by the continuing width equals 4.5, even. Here then is the redundancy statement to emphasize the 1.5 figure identified earlier by the pit passage cutoff. Even more emphatic because it is a double redundancy!!

$$3 + 1.5 = 4.5$$
$$3 \times 1.5 = 4.5$$

And, of course, the noble number 2 times 1.5 equals "three."
5. Finally, its drop times the passage width equals 1.5, exactly. To state it succinctly, 1.5 is a very important fact, according to the designer.

Just in case the initiate missed the full impact of 1.5, it is repeated in the next step of instruction, and again related to the noble 2 number. The remaining distance from the "three" passage floor discontinuity to the East-West centerline of the pyramid is 12.43083346 units (25 ft. 8 2/3 in. or 7840.30 mm); which centerline, not just incidently, is also the centerline of the Queen's Chamber. Dividing this distance by 1.5 equals 8.287222307 units (17 ft. 1 25/32 in. or 5226.86 mm) for the length of the final Queen's Chamber passage.

Continuity of design now carries on in the Queen's Chamber itself. The remaining distance to the centerline of both the pyramid and the chamber is 4.143611154 units (8 ft. 6 57/64 in. or 2613.43 mm). This, of course, is the half width of the chamber and half length of the final passage. Thus, the final passage length and chamber width are the same; or to put it another way, two times either dimension equals the distance between the passage discontinuity to the South wall of the Queen's Chamber.

Design continuity proceeds from the chamber width to its length very simply. The width divided by the discontinuity drop equals the East-West length of the Queen's Chamber of 9.108879797 units (18 ft. 10 3/16 in. or 5745.10 mm). As a point of interest, this length fails to reach the vertical centerline of the pyramid by 3.274499089 units (81 5/16 in. or 2065.27 mm).

Lifting his attention from the floor the initiate would instinctively expect this continuity to progress into the third or vertical dimension of this chamber; but this is not the case. If it were, the designer could simply use a flat ceiling at a proper height. Instead, a gabled ceiling meets the eye. Its ridge line runs East and West exactly along this central vertical cross-section of the Great Pyramid. In fact, in looking at the East or West ends of the chamber, the walls form an arrow shape pointing up toward the half area level yet to be reached. So, rather than a single third dimension, a dual dimension is discovered: The height of the ceiling at the top of the North and South walls and the height of the ridge. This presents a greater challenge.

The East wall is the key to the solution of this chamber's mystery, for it contains the Niche within its dimensions. This distinctive feature has three characteristics of initial interest: Its outline shape is rather like five boxes or blocks stacked up in order of diminishing size, its depth of recess is uniformly the same as the width of the three passages used to get here, and its centerline is located off-center to the right or South of the common chamber and pyramid centerline section. These are the clues to be studied further, since the shape is not a logical one for a human statue, the depth is a fourth repeat of a precise number, and the logic of the location is not obvious.

What is obvious is the designer's intent to get the initiate to sit well back in the chamber to contemplate the design of the East wall and Niche, and to learn therefrom. After studying the situation for some time, the initiate is suddenly aware of the Niche solution and the significance of the knowledge it conveys.

Time and again the mind's eye sees a solution, each of which recedes in significance as a breaker on a beach when it doesn't reach a high-water mark of significance, in this case design continuity relevance. But like the surf, repetition almost becomes hypnotic. Repetition, or redundancy, there is a key that snaps the mind back to higher

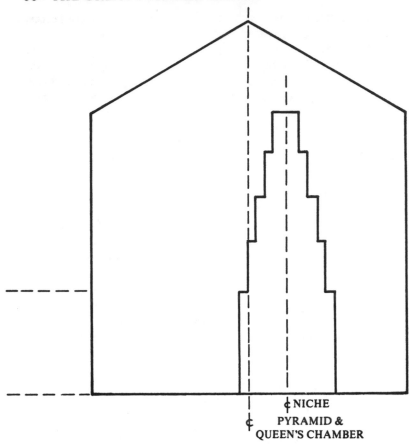

Fig. 7-1. Queen's Chamber East Wall with Recessed Niche.

levels of insight. What is the significance of the same dimension for widths of the descending and ascending "pi" passages, the width of the "three" passage and the depth of the Niche? And, as the initiate is soon to find, the square entrance to the King's Chamber, just in case it were overlooked along the way? Yes, square this dimension of 1.648721271 and it is found to be equal to 2.718281828, or exactly equal to "e," the base of the natural (Naperian) logarithm system. Here then is another constant known to the designer. In mathematics it is the limit to which the expression $(1 + 1/n)^n$ reaches as n becomes very large. Strange as it may seem at first, the use of "e" often simplifies resolution of higher mathematical expressions, such as in the calculus, and is often found as a function in the natural sciences; pressure related to altitude, for example.

With this discovery stimulating the mind, the Niche becomes the focus of renewed interest. Look at it again through fresh eyes. Instead of seeing five discrete rectangular configurations, suppose the designer sought to express an integrated simple curvilinear figure in rectilinear format, as is the whole Great Pyramid design. Now instead of seeing the Niche as outlined in Fig. 7-1, the mind's eye sees it as:

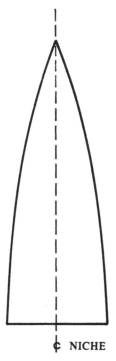

Fig. 7-2. Queen's Chamber Niche as Curvilinear Visualization.

Immediately, associations come to mind: a projectile, a spaceship, an arrowhead, a cathedral window; or a half of a flying saucer, a lens, a pillow, a cissoid, and so on. Eventually, speculative associations give way to the desire to know. If this configuration were the central intent of the designer, it would be centrally located within the East wall. Since it is not, it more logically assumes the position of a step in the teaching and learning process. Thus, besides the open question of the two Chamber heights represented by the wall, we now have two additional queries as to the particular size and location of the Niche itself.

Regardless of the degradations of time, surely the hard outlines of the Niche reveal the design intent. First, it should be remembered, the designer preferred the language of theoretical simplicity for purity of message transmission, using recognizable complexities such as "e" as verification of both proper translation and degree of knowledge transmission. In other words, if the value and use of "e" were unknown to the observer, he would have no way to prove design intent, nor to understand the extent of the designer's knowledge. Again, the design is intended to teach rather than to obscure some particular fact. This being so, the visualized Niche curves are found to be simple circular curves rather than more complex elliptical curves or indefinable curves.

Even though the rectilinear Niche and its curvilinear basis are fact and theory combined, the simplest approach is to separate them and start with the facts, or what is actually observed. The first or lowest rectangular figure was designed so the base of the Niche horizontal dimension is 2.5 units (62 5/64 inches or 1576.78 mm) and its height is 2 2/3 units (66 7/32 inches or 1681.90 mm). Its area, therefore, equals 6 2/3 units squared or 10/1.5, and the volume equals 10.99147514 units cubed or $10\sqrt{e}/1.5$, a variation of an already familiar number, the reciprocal of the Queen's Chamber passage step times ten. This may not seem too important yet, but with only one rectangular shape the designer sought to impress upon the mind of the initiate three important numbers: 10 as the base of the decimal system, e as the base of the natural logarithm system, and 1.5 a previously discovered number (overall Great Pyramid depth) as the base of a system yet to be determined. In addition, if the area is squared, the number 44.44444444 is derived, which equals 1000/22.5 or $10^3/22.5$, which also equals $10^2/2.25$ or $10^2/1.5^2$, for another interrelationship. The two circles overlapping by 2.5 units to form the theoretical curvilinear Niche each have a radius of exactly 22.5 units.

Along the top side of the first rectangular shape the sides of the Niche jut inward as two shoulders to define the base dimension of the second rectangular shape. Each of these first shoulders, however, does not stop at the visualized curvilinear shape as might be expected. Instead, they exceed the expected shoulder width. To avoid the complications of calculation as this procedure repeats up through the stack, the important findings are listed, in units only, in the following tables. This tabulation is in order of decreasing rectangular size ascending as the initiate's gaze would travel up the Niche to the fifth pair of shoulders that join to form the top of the Niche. Table 7-1 lists the factual face dimensions and Table 7-2 provides the derived information or lesson material.

Table 7-1. Design Face Dimensions of the Niche.

Rectangle	Dimension	Value	Notes
#1	Width	2.500000000	$5/2 = 2\ 1/2$
	Height	2.666666667	$8/3 = 2\ 2/3$
	Sum of Heights	2.666666667	
	Circle Shoulder	.1585835500	$\times\ 1.454402515 =$
	Actual Shoulder	.2306443140	Actual
#2	Width	2.038711371	$.75\ e = 5\ V_2/V_1$
	Height	1.333333333	$4/3 = 1\ 1/3$
	Sum of Heights	4.000000000	$2^2 = 4$
	Circle Shoulder	.1277658560	$\times\ 1.526190616 =$
	Actual Shoulder	.1949950505	Actual
#3	Width	1.648721271	$\sqrt{e} = e^{0.5}$
	Height	1.170585214	$(10/V_1)^2\sqrt{2} = V_3/e$
	Sum of Heights	5.170585214	
	Circle Shoulder	.1765285855	$\times\ 1.473973290 =$
	Actual Shoulder	.2601984200	Actual
#4	Width	1.128324431	
	Height	1.140315491	
	Sum of Heights	6.310900705	
	Circle Shoulder	.2173445733	$\times\ 1.000000000 =$
	Actual Shoulder	.2173445733	Actual
#5	Width	.6936352843	
	Height	1.084199024	
	Sum of Heights	7.395099729	
	Circle Shoulder	.3468176422	$\times\ 1.000000000 =$
	Actual Shoulder	.3468176422	Actual

Table 7-2. Derived information from the Niche.

Rectangle	Dimension	Item	Value	Equivalent
#1	2nd	Area	6.666666667	$20/3 = 6\ 2/3 = 10/1.5$
	3rd	Volume	10.99147514	$10\sqrt{e}/1.5 = 10\ (\sqrt{e}/1.5)$
	4th	Area²	44.44444444	$1000/22.5 = 10^3/22.5 = 10^2/2.25 = 10^2/1.5^2$
	5th	(A) (V)	73.27650093	$10^2\ \sqrt{e}/1.5^2$
#2	2nd	Area	2.718281828	$e^1 = e$
	3rd	Volume	4.481689070	$e^{1.5}$
	4th	Area²	7.389056096	e^2
	5th	(A) (V)	12.18249396	$e^{2.5}$
#3	2nd	Area	1.929968741	$1.5^2\ \sqrt{2}/e = 1.5\ \sqrt{4.5}/e = \sqrt{10.125}/e = 9/\sqrt{8}e$
	3rd	Volume	3.181980516	$1.5^2\ \sqrt{2} = 1.5\ \sqrt{4.5} = \sqrt{10.125} = 9/\sqrt{8}$

4th	Area^2	3.724779341	$1.5^4(2)/e = 1.5^2(4.5)/e = 10.125/e = 81/8e$
5th	(A) (V)	6.141122928	$1.5^4(2)/\sqrt{e} = 1.5^2(4.5)/\sqrt{e} = 10.125/\sqrt{e} = 81/8\sqrt{e}$

#4

2nd	Area	1.286645827	$1.5 \sqrt{2}/e = \sqrt{4.5}/e$
3rd	Volume	2.121320343	$1.5 \sqrt{2} = \sqrt{4.5} = 12/2^{2.5}$
4th	Area^2	1.655457484	$1.5^2(2)/e = 4.5/e$
5th	(A) (V)	2.729387968	$1.5^2(2)/\sqrt{e} = 4.5/\sqrt{e}$

#5

2nd	Area	.7520386981	$\ln 1.5\sqrt{2} = \ln \sqrt{4.5} = \ln 1.5 + \ln \sqrt{2}$
3rd	Volume	1.239902198	$\ln (\sqrt{4.5})^{\sqrt{e}} = \sqrt{e} \ln \sqrt{4.5}$
4th	Area^2	.5655622034	$\ln^2 1.5\sqrt{2} = \ln^2 \sqrt{4.5}$
5th	(A) (V)	.9324544361	$\sqrt{e} \ln^2 1.5\sqrt{2} = \sqrt{e} \ln^2 \sqrt{4.5}$

Truly, we have a learning center which, by use of a few established numerical relationships combined with whole number relationships, progressively teaches the mathematical law of exponents and logarithms. The design of this three-dimensional crossword puzzle itself covers a broad spectrum of higher mathematical functions; a single example is rectangular to polar coordinate conversion.

The use of 22.5 units for the radii of the circles proves numerically interesting in several ways also. First, it is equal to both 10×1.5^2 and 15×1.5, both using the important 1.5 base noted previously. Secondly, by division, it produces Niche related numbers or whole numbers:

$$\frac{22.5}{1.25} = 18$$

$$\frac{22.5}{1.5} = 15$$

$$\frac{22.5}{2.25} = 10$$

$$\frac{22.5}{2.5} = 9$$

$$\frac{22.5}{3} = 7.5$$

$$\frac{22.5}{3.375} = \frac{22.5}{1.5^3} = \frac{20}{3} = 6.666666667$$

$$\frac{22.5}{4.5} = 5$$

$$\frac{22.5}{5.0625} = \frac{22.5}{1.5^4} = \frac{1}{.225} = 4.444444444$$

And thirdly, it proves interesting trigonometrically as:

$$\text{Tan } 22.5° = .4142135624 = \sqrt{2} - 1$$
$$\text{Cot } 22.5° = 2.4142135624 = \sqrt{2} + 1$$
$$\frac{22.5°}{90°} = .25 = \frac{1}{4}$$
$$\frac{22.5°}{360°} = .0625 = \frac{1}{16}$$

Leaving this numerical diversion to return to the main inquiry, the initiate's attention returns to the final Queen's Chamber design question to be resolved; that is, the relationship of the Niche position in the East wall to the chamber's two heights. In short order, after another look at the now defined Niche and its position, the mind's eye sees the obvious.

The designer knew that just three points define a circular curve, and so just three points define each Niche circle; the ends of the base line, the fourth shoulder projections, and, of course, the center of the height where the fifth shoulders meet. Now watch as the two curves are projected further upward.

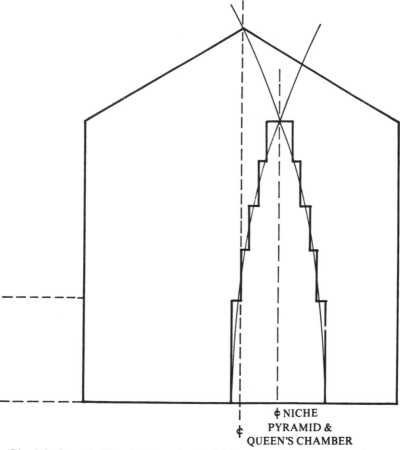

¢ NICHE
¢ PYRAMID &
QUEEN'S CHAMBER

Fig. 7-3. Queen's Chamber East Wall with Recessed Niche Showing Overlapping Circles of Niche Design Extended.

With the Fig. 7-3 visualization, it becomes immediately apparent the height of the Niche is directly related to the minimum height of the chamber, and by projection related to the maximum chamber height. The Niche height and minimum chamber height are the same at 7.395099729 units (15 ft. 3 5/8 in. or 4664.19 mm) regardless of the Niche location in the East wall. Where it is located determines the maximum chamber height by the left-hand circle projection. So why is the Niche positioned precisely where it is?

Here again first suggested solutions do not prove out. Since the centerline of the pyramid and chamber pass through the left first shoulder rather than along the left side of the second rectangle, the latter was not a position criterion. That the maximum height was a simple predetermination such as π^2 units is also disproved by precise position. Eventually, position by proportion takes root in the initiate's train of thought. And again, not a simple proportion such as the ϕ proportion. After determining what the precise Niche position is not, the mind is cleared to think as the designer reasoned: The teaching of the Niche design is important, so do not detract from it with extraneous information; use its circular design to establish precise proportional position.

The answer relies on three points: the left circle intersection of the pyramid and chamber centerline, the two circle intersection at the centerline of the Niche, and the right circle intersection of the right-hand chamber ceiling line. The latter two were used to determine the first. That is, in simple terminology, make the two-part proportioning of the right-hand chamber ceiling line the same as the two-part proportioning of the chamber width by the centerline of the Niche. The major proportion of each turns out to be a .6219114037 ratio to the whole of either. This ratio then determines the centerline of the Niche to be 1.010306904 units (25 3/32 in. or 637.21 mm) South of the centerline of the pyramid and chamber. It also determines the maximum height of the chamber to be 9.828775264 units (20 ft. 4 1/16 in. or 6199.14 mm). One further calculation shows the design ceiling slopes of the Queen's Chamber to be 30.42708053° (30° 25' 37.490").

A moment of reflection shows the Queen's Chamber and passage are related to, but not part of, the message encoded in the design of the Great Pyramid. Even the Niche says so by not being on the centerline of the pyramid, but including it within its outlines. Indeed, this digression from the main design is a learning center, and the initiate learns that the designer knew far more than history credits him. The ancient wisdom imparted here confirms the extent of pre-history knowledge and intent to preserve a permanent message in stone, for those whose knowledge has begun again to reach the designer's level. And, as you prepare to leave this learning center, remember that you still have much to learn, including the importance of 1.5 as the base of a system yet to be determined.

VIII. HALL OF LIGHT

Retracing his steps to the juncture of the "three" passage and the ascending "pi" passage, but before looking upward to study the Grand Gallery, the initiate looks down the ascending passage toward the plug blocks. Yes, there are points of interest there, not to be overlooked. These points are the "girdle stones" found at regular intervals equal to the width of the Queen's Chamber. An interesting fact to remember as you turn completely around, lift up your eyes and scan the extensive enlargement of the upper half of the ascending "pi" passage.

The ascending passage slope amplifies both the feeling of length and height of the Grand Gallery. In fact, the feeling of height is intensified by the seven corbelled, or stepped-inward, sections of the upper two-thirds of the side walls. These seven steps reduce the maximum width so that the highest width is again the same as the "pi" passage width at the floor level, or as you will recall, equal to the square root of e. This then leaves seven other widths, the maximum plus the intervening six corbels, to be described. The multiple widths of the Grand Gallery were not the designer's chief concern, however. With this awareness comes the question of what was.

After this initial scan and query, one slowly begins to realize a subtle design transition within the immediate impression of grandeur. All of the lines of length are parallel to the floor, or ascending slope, with no lines of height normal, or perpendicular, to them. The lines of height are all vertical. This deviates from the usual rectangular mode of expression, and yet, it springs forth from the continuation of the defined "pi" passage. Apparently, the designer wanted to continue one plane of thought while introducing another.

As the initiate stands on the level open section of the "three" passage floor contemplating the specifics of the Grand Gallery, several mental notes are made. Not only does the gallery widen to its maximum at exactly the half height of the ascending "pi" passage, it also overextends the culmination of its alloted proportion of the "pi" passage at both gallery ends.

At its beginning, or North lowest face, the Grand Gallery starts .6907259479 units (17 5/32 inches or 435.65 mm) of "pi" passage floor measurement before it reaches the theoretical juncture with the "three" passage floor level. Or put another way, the lowest North wall section of the gallery is .6191247034 units (15 3/8 inches or 390.49 mm) further North than expected. Why this is so becomes clear when it is observed that the junction of the top of the "pi" passage with its portion of the North gallery wall is at exactly the same level as the top of the "three" passage.

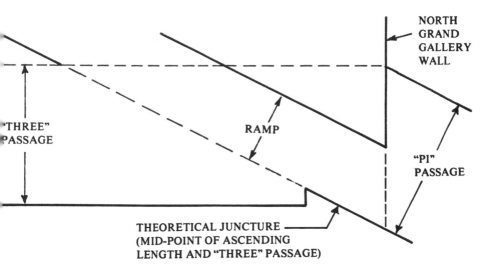

Fig. 8-1. Cross-Section of the North (Lower) End of the Grand Gallery.

In visualizing the cross-section of the North (lower) end of the Grand Gallery as shown in Fig. 8-1, the initiate sees the important key to the cross-section design intent: Measure Grand Gallery heights vertically!

Even the "three" passage lip reinforces this discovery. If the ramp length is measured along its upward slope from its start at the gallery

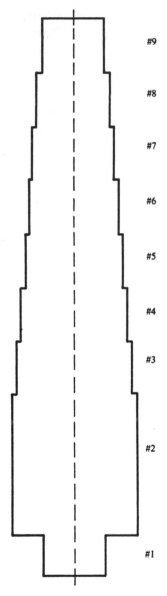

#9

#8

#7

#6

#5

#4

#3

#2

#1

Fig. 8-2. Vertical Cross-Section of Grand Gallery.

North wall to the top level of the "three" passage, then halved, a point is located directly above the height of the lip, which is .2252130980 units (5 19/32 inches or 142.04 mm). This also checks against measuring the ascending floor length from the North wall to the lip height, then proceeding along the ascending floor line that far again, which is a point level with the start of the ramp.

Since the designer indicates vertical measurement of the gallery, rather than perpendicular to the floor, it becomes convenient to check the Grand Gallery cross-section with the handy North wall. At the half "pi" passage height, where the gallery expands across the surface of the side ramps to its maximum width, the width of each ramp is .8243606355 units (20 15/32 inches or 519.94 mm). The sum of the two ramps widths, 1.648721271 units, equals $\sqrt{e}$, which is also the width of both the "pi" passage and the "three" passage. Thus, the second, and widest, section of the gallery is $2\sqrt{e}$ wide, or four times a ramp width.

The vertical height of this second section from the ramp surface up to the first corbel is 3.639183958 units (90 23/64 inches or 2295.28 mm). This is equal to six divided by the square root of e. Thus, the area of the second section equals $2\sqrt{e}$ times $6/\sqrt{e}$, or 12 square units. Since this is exactly four times the "three" passage cross-section area, you immediately recall the "three" passage dimensions and realize the width and height of this section are each exactly double those of the "three" passage. Here is another confirmation of vertical measurement.

Obviously, subtracting the width of section #9 ($\sqrt{e}$) from the width of section #2 ($2\sqrt{e}$) leaves a difference of $\sqrt{e}$. Dividing this difference by two times the seven corbels (or 14) shows each corbel to be $\sqrt{e}/14$, equal to .1177658051 units (2 59/64 inches or 74.28 mm).

With each corbelled section height found to be identical, only one further measurement need be noted. This dimension is 1.413189661 units (35 1/64 inches or 891.32 mm), which equal $6\sqrt{e}/7$. Now the initiate may tabulate the basic vertical cross-sections of the Grand Gallery as shown in Table 8-1.

Basic Section	Design Width	Basis Vert. Ht.	Area Basis	Area Units²	Related To:
#1	$\sqrt{e}$	$\pi/2\sqrt{e}\ \mathrm{Cos}\ A$	$\pi/2\ \mathrm{Cos}\ A$	1.752457583	"π" Passage
#2	$2\sqrt{e}$	$6/\sqrt{e}$	12	12.00000000	"3" Passage
#3	$13\sqrt{e}/7$	$6\sqrt{e}/7$	78 e/49	4.327060869	e
#4	$12\sqrt{e}/7$	$6\sqrt{e}/7$	72 e/49	3.994210033	e
#5	$11\sqrt{e}/7$	$6\sqrt{e}/7$	66 e/49	3.661359196	e
#6	$10\sqrt{e}/7$	$6\sqrt{e}/7$	60 e/49	3.328508361	e
#7	$9\sqrt{e}/7$	$6\sqrt{e}/7$	54 e/49	2.995657524	e
#8	$8\sqrt{e}/7$	$6\sqrt{e}/7$	48 e/49	2.662806688	e
#9	$\sqrt{e}$	$6\sqrt{e}/7$	6 e/7	2.329955853	e

Table 8-1. Design Basis for Vertical Cross-Section of Grand Gallery.

So, the Grand Gallery begins by relating to three internal identifications, (pi, three, and e) found within the Great Pyramid up to this point, and in the order of discovery. Here again is confirming reiteration combined with step-by-small-step progression wisely designed to impress the correctness of interpretation in the mind of the initiate. Table 8-1 also points to progress, which becomes more apparent after a simplifying mental sketch is made of the corbelled sections #3 through #9.

Obviously, the designer wanted to introduce six (as 6, 12 and 1/12) and seven (as 7, 14 and 1/7) into your vocabulary at this time. Also, reidentified are our old friends two and its reciprocal, one half. In haste, one might say a series of fractions or decimal equivalents do not add up to much, but they do—although, of course, it is not that obvious.

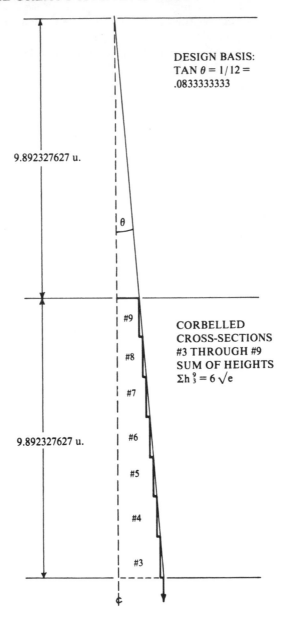

Fig. 8-3. Design Basis for the Corbelled Sections of the Grand Gallery.

Remember the reciprocal of the Queen's Chamber ratio, the square root of e divided by 1.5? Remember how this ratio was repeated times ten as the volume of the first level of the Niche? Here was a decimal number multiplied by the base of the common decimal system as redundancy confirmation. The corbelled section of the Grand Gallery performs a similar proof of deliberate intent too. The vertical basic cross-section #9 is 2.329955853, while the sum of cross-sections #3 through #9 is 23.29955853! Again, the factor of 10 appears.

Likewise, you may have noticed in Fig. 8-3 the summation of the corbelled sections' heights, which was mathematically noted as $\Sigma\, h\,{}^{9}_{3} = 6\sqrt{e}$. When this is read as the sum of heights from #3 to #9 equals ...you are reading the introduction to integral calculus. Thus, with a simple grandeur, the designer calls the initiate's attention to two summations, each with a point to make, one confirming and one progressing.

There is, however, another point being made here also. What about the "six" and "seven" words of the vocabulary? Look up at the corbelled section again. You see seven sections. Seven is a whole number, a real number, an odd number, a positive number, and a prime number. Now look back to Fig. 8-3, and above the seven real steps, you can see in your mind seven imaginary identical steps to the design apex or origin, or zero point, if you prefer. But, to those who only speak of numbers by counting on their fingers, zero is a new concept. Historically, this is true, for our notation of nought came from India in the ninth century A.D. via Arab traders. "As ssifr," a cipher, therefore is relatively recent in written form, although the Maya culture may have noted it a few centuries sooner. But, long before either, the Great Pyramid points it out with a simple equation involving limits.

For a moment, return to depth rather than height point of view. If you visualize the uppermost actual corbelled cross-section as number zero, you can count each section downward to the limit of +6. Counting the imaginary sections upward to the Grand Gallery design apex, you reach −7 as the limit. With each section, n, so numbered, and the setting constant "a" equal to seven, the simple formula for the area of any of these sections becomes:

$$\text{C.S. Area}_n = \frac{e\,(a + n)\,(a - 1)}{a^2}\ ,\quad \text{Limits: } n = +6 \text{ and } -7$$

Or, if you wish to use the other vocabulary word, six, as the constant "b" the simple cross-section formula for any section becomes:

C.S. Area$_n$ = $\dfrac{e\,(b+1+n)\,(b)}{(b+1)^2}$,   Limits: n = +6 and −7

Actually, this point uses two new vocabulary words to introduce the concepts of zero, positive and negative, and a series with limits. Here again, the last of these is useful in the introduction of elementary concepts for teaching integral calculus. As usual, the designer does not let the initiate assume this may have been coincidental, or unintentional. Positive intent shows up as a single step to a simple basic relationship for intent confirmation: The sum of the visible cross-sections (23.29955853) divided by the sum of the imaginary cross-sections (6.989867558) equals 3.333333333, or ten divided by three, both of which are previously identified and used words spoken by the Great Pyramid design.

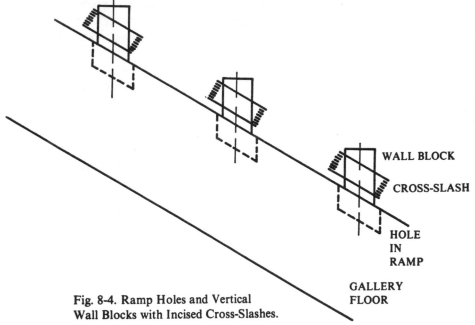

WALL BLOCK

CROSS-SLASH

HOLE
IN
RAMP

GALLERY
FLOOR

Fig. 8-4. Ramp Holes and Vertical
Wall Blocks with Incised Cross-Slashes.

After all this concentrated mental exercise, the Grand Gallery now offers a welcome change of pace—the physical exercise of negotiating the remaining ascending slope. As the initiate ascends, he becomes aware of a series of pairs of shallow, rectangular "post-holes" along the outer edges of the ramps. The west hole of the first pair is now missing with its ramp section at the upper terminus of the well shaft. Regardless, however, 27 pairs of these vertical, but top- and bottom-sloped, holes were designed into the ramps. Even though their purpose is not apparent at this point, these empty holes do hold a passing interest. The fact that they are uniform pairs and regularly spaced between themselves, but not the ends of the ramps, shows design intent for a purpose not directly related to the primary ramp length design. The holes themselves are of $\sqrt{e}$ divided by 2 or .8243606355 units slope length (20 15/32 inches or 519.94 mm) with twice that as interval spacing. In other words, the holes to one another are on 1.5$\sqrt{e}$, or 2.473081907 units (61 13/32 inches or 1559.81 mm), center-to-center spacing along the wall sides of the ramps. Here again are two words, 1.5 and $\sqrt{e}$, previously identified and used by the Great Pyramid design. The 1.5 word is becoming of great interest now because of its repeated use and as yet unidentified significance.

As Fig. 8-4 shows, there are a number of dimensions involved with the ramp holes and their attendant vertical wall blocks with incised cross-slashes. A brief summary list is as follows:

Dimension	Measurement	Value (Units)	Equivalent
Hole Length	Slope	.8243606355	$\sqrt{e}/2$
Hole Centers	Slope	2.473081907	1.5$\sqrt{e}$
Hole Depth	Vertical	.4054651081	ln 1.5
Hole Width	Across	.2413353867	2/LC width
Block Height	Center	.8243606355	$\sqrt{e}/2$
Block Width	Horizontal	.5248042801	$\sqrt{e}/\pi$
Slash Length	Slope	1.000000000	1
Slash Width	$\perp$ Slope	.3183098861	$1/\pi$
Slash to Ramp	$\perp$ Slope	.1591549431	$1/2\pi$

Having noted the ramp holes, and that their pair spacing is not directly related to the primary ramp length design, recall your attention as an initiate to the subject of the Grand Gallery length. Because of the Great Step looming up ahead and the upper level corbels, the proper design term is lengths. While negotiating the ascending slope, the initiate is allowed the opportunity to learn the slope length as cataloged in Table 8-2. Since the Great Step riser denotes the east-west cross-section centerline of the pyramid, the table lists slope length total by ascending levels and amount both north and south of this centerline.

Level	Length in Units	North Portion	South Portion
#1	70.34163205	70.34163205	0.000000000
#2	73.12109677	70.34163205	2.779464724
#3	72.98971145	70.34163205	2.648079404
#4	72.72694081	70.21024673	2.516694084
#5	72.46417017	70.07886141	2.385308764
#6	72.20139953	69.94747609	2.253923444
#7	71.93862889	69.81609077	2.122538124
#8	71.67585825	69.68470545	1.991152804
#9	71.41308761	69.55332013	1.859767484

Table 8-2. Slope Lengths of the Nine Grand Gallery Levels.

In looking at the highest level (#9), the initiate finds another design feature of the Grand Gallery. This level is sub-divided by 36 ceiling blocks each notched down into the side walls of this level. As far as construction is concerned, this rack arrangement has the definite advantage of anchoring each block and the weight of the stone above it to prevent down-slope slippage. In other words, this saw-tooth design would theoretically allow removal of a single block with the other 35 remaining stationary. But, from the floor of the Grand Gallery, the complexities of this design which is far above us shall remain of less concern to the initiate than the simple observation of the number of ceiling blocks: The 36 ceiling blocks are related to the 27 pairs of ramp holes eight levels apart by the reiteration of the 1.5 mystery word spoken so often.

$$(36)\,(1.5) = 54 = (27)\,(2)$$

$$\text{or } \frac{(27)\,(2)}{36} = 1.5$$

Between the ceiling and ramps appears one more feature of note. This consists of an incised groove running the length of the fifth cross-section (third corbel) along each side of the Grand Gallery. These .03-unit (3/4 inch or 19 mm) deep by .24-unit (6 inches or 152 mm) high grooves are located at the mid-point level between the ramp surface and the serrated ceiling. If you were viewing the Grand Gallery from the side, as shown in Figure 8-5, the inverse form of the 1.5 relationship is amplified as:

36 ceiling blocks

—— groove ——

54 ramp holes

As the initiate approaches the deteriorated Great Step, a sense of suspense and anticipation starts to build. The riser, or vertical portion, of the step is right on the east-west centerline cross-section of the Great Pyramid itself and is the end-point of the two Grand Gallery side ramps. Its height is 1.470887340 units (36 17/32 inches or 927.71 mm) from the floor and .4079680860 units (10 1/8 inches or 257.31 mm) above the ends of the side ramp surfaces.

The level top of the Great Step is at the half area depth of the Great Pyramid and measures across the same as the width of the Grand Gallery #2 level of 3.297442542 units (81 7/8 inches or 2079.74 mm), which is equal to two times the square root of e. Its length from the riser edge to the south end wall of the gallery is 2.491343026 units (61 55/64 inches or 1571.32 mm). The only obvious feature of this surface area is a pair of side holes in the south corners. These are similar to the ramp holes, but not the same: The width is the same, but without the wall block or cross-slash; the depth is less at only one third of a unit; the length is the same at one half the square root of e, except here it is horizontal instead of slope measured and delineates the horizontal sum of the seven corbel offsets directly above.

But where is the long-promised great significance of this juncture? An undercurrent of anxiety is felt. Did you miss a vital clue along the way? It is almost as if you had stepped over the threshold of significance. What happened? You bend over to peer into the First Low Passage leading onward through the south wall of the Grand Gallery. You see only that it is a square with both height and width of the square root of e units and a length of 2.148855597 units (53 23/64 inches or 1355.31 mm). This is the same width as the other significant

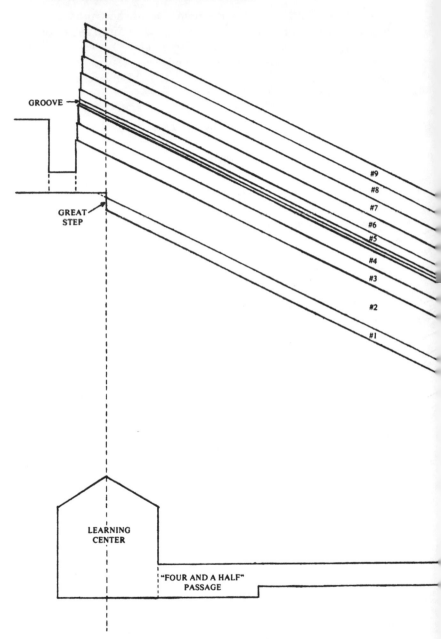

Fig. 8-5. Cross-Section of Grand Gallery Length.

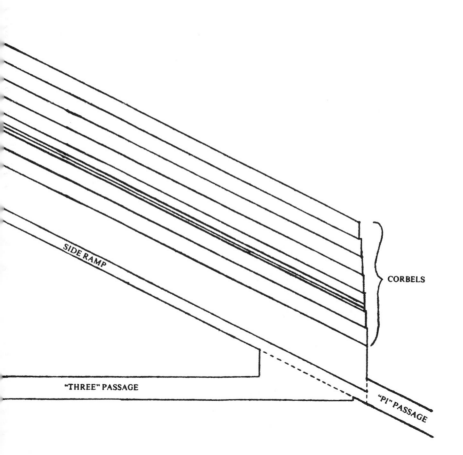

passages, but is an "e" passage in cross-section area. The designer certainly liked the words "e" and "1.5," but why? When in doubt, think as the designer thought.

This pinnacle upon which the initiate finds himself has to be the key turning point of the whole design. The Great Step must be the pivotal point of the message for it juts into the continuity of the lines of thought so carefully and precisely established up to this promontory position. In looking back down the Grand Gallery from the Great Step, the serration of the ceiling and the ramp holes seem to pale in the perspective of the vast rush of unbroken lines of sight sweeping up to and past the brink of this step. The "pi" passage looks remote, yet remindful of something. Oh, yes, design intent.

Look back through the mind's eye to Fig. 8-5, Cross-Section of Grand Gallery Length, and you begin to see the design effect of the Great Step. If the "pi" passage and Grand Gallery floor line were not interrupted by the step, it would cross the half area level floor line .4822831280 units (11 31/32 inches or 304.18 mm) inside of the "e" passage entrance. And, if this imaginary segment were continued, it would bisect the "e" passage height at its southern end. Likewise, were the half vertical height line of the "pi" passage and ramp surface continued, it would cross the step surface at .8247705568 units (20 31/64 inches or 520.19 mm) south of the lip and bisect the "e" passage height at its northern end. So, as the floor measurement stops at the base of the Great Step, we are taught to raise our sights to the half passage height level which is where the ramp surfaces terminate against the step riser. Thus, we now see the "recorded in stone" total folded "pi" passage floor length of 311.4883214 units lifted vertically to the *central passage position.* Recalling the fact of the descending "pi" passage pointing as a lens-less telescope at the North pole star, which would send a beam of light straight down the *central passage position,* snaps the design intent into focus with the speed of light. The startled initiate has just heard the Great Pyramid speak and stands in disbelief. Its message, "Look to (at) a star (which is) 311.4883214 light-years (distance) from the earth."

"Incredible" is your immediate reaction; but is it? The designer knew you would not believe he had knowledge far more precise than our best today. And yet, he did design the Great Pyramid to speak to you and to advise you of the prehistoric existence of a more advanced culture or civilization. Still pulling yourself together after this startling revelation, you want the designer to prove it to you beyond a

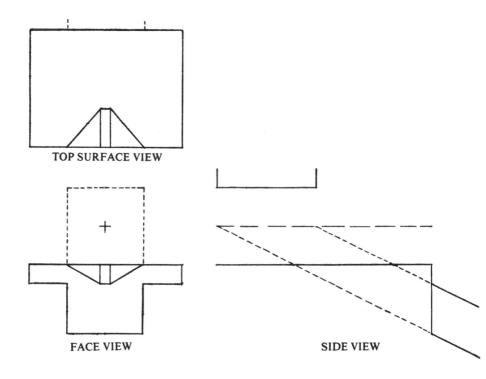

TOP SURFACE VIEW

FACE VIEW

SIDE VIEW

Fig. 8-6. Views of Great Step Showing Oblique Slot

reasonable doubt. This is foolish, for he believed what he recorded; it is up to you, the initiate, to prove it to yourself. *How* is by the same use of logic that got you to this point. Use your head, but feel the Great Step with your feet. Did the designer foresee the extent of the central lip deterioration, or has his Fig. 8-6 design been defaced and overlooked?

In visualizing Fig. 8-6, Views of Great Step Showing Oblique Slot, the first proof of the Great Pyramid message is perceived. As can be seen, the valley floor centrally follows the same slope line as the side ramp surfaces and would have been found to be as wide as one half of the riser distance from ramp to lip. The maximum valley width was identical to the Grand Gallery #1 level width and tapered to the valley floor conjunction with the step surface. Now, what is the importance of this oblique slot?

Think back over your initiation to the point of finding the plug blocks at the entrance to the ascending "pi" passage. Did you see even a pin-hole drilled centrally through these blocks? No, you did not because this was never an operating observatory in which an actual beam of star-light could be admitted, amplified and projected toward the beam-splitter. If you can, imagine a laser aimed along the central axis at the terminus of the "pi" passage with its .2039840430 unit (5 1/16 inch or 128.66 mm) diameter beam of parallel light rays pointed at the beam-splitter. You would then see a slightly semi-elliptical spot of light on the riser face immediately below the lip of the valley floor. The upper would appear to sit upon the central axis cross-bar shown in the Fig. 8-6 Face View if a screen were placed at the entrance to the "e" passage. In the Fig. 8-6 Side View you can see that without an entrance screen an elongated semi-elliptical spot of light would appear on the ceiling of the "e" passage near its southern end. Thus, the lower half of the beam would terminate on the Great Step riser at the east-west central axis of the pyramid while the upper half would terminate in the "e" passage denoting the end of this line of thought. One additional note of interest in looking at the Fig. 8-6 Face View is its resemblance to a truncated, stylized humanoid form: The split-beam projection would then focus half on the heart area and half on penetrating the mind.

Now that a beam-splitter has introduced the initiate to the concept of light traveling and being observed at a particular place or places, what additional backup evidence may be found for a second proof? Again, think back over your initiation. The designer liked the words "e" and "1.5," with the former signifying a value, a logarithm or an exponent. To go directly to the point being made, look down the Grand Gallery: You see the big *1.5* spelled out all the way to the northern end wall. *Crosswise* is the wall area which is saying that the sum of corbelled sections three through nine is *ten* times number nine. How far up to the origin from the floor is nine real sections plus seven imaginary sections for a count of *16*? Pick up the *italicized* words and place them so:

$$1.5 \times 10^{16}$$

This enormous number (15,000,000,000,000,000) can also be written as 15×10^{15} if it is easier to remember. If you have this many units and the Great Pyramid is designed to the precise solar year, as surely as the light dawns every day of that year, the Great Pyramid unit of measure is based on the speed of light, a universal constant! The second proof, then, consists of a statement that the designer believed the speed of light to be 1.5×10^{16} units per solar year. This converts to current terminology as 475,331,468 units per second which is equivalent to 186,286 miles per second or 299,798,057 meters per second. Compare this to the "latest correction" reported on page 4 of the *Chicago Daily News* dated September 9, 1974, as 299,792,459 meters per second. In percentage difference you find 0.0019% to be very small indeed.

For a third proof, the designer points to the North polar star and has the Great Pyramid say 311.4883214 units. Is he identifying the star by light-year distance from the earth? Due to precession, the axis of the earth points in the direction of a different star in successive ages of the 25,800-year cycle. This very gradual shifting can best be appreciated as displayed in Table 8-3 since it takes centuries to approach and leave each star in turn. Because both the intervals and precession are irregular, the date is shown as a rounded number.

Approx. Date	Common Star Name	Constellation	Actual Designation	True North Proximity
2,500 BC	Thuban	Draco	alpha Draconis	Close
2,000 AD	Polaris	Ursa Minor	alpha Ursae Minoris	Fair
4,000 AD	Er Rai	Cepheus	gamma Cephei	Fair
10,000 AD	Deneb	Cygnus	alpha Cygni	Poor
14,000 AD	Vega	Lyra	alpha Lyrae	Poor

Table 8-3. Apparent Movement of the North Celestial Pole.

Considering the fact that the Golden Age of pyramid construction in Egypt spanned a relatively short period of 120 years from 2680 BC to 2560 BC, attention is focused on alpha Draconis. However, to keep the five pole stars listed in Table 8-3 in perspective, look at what modern astronomic tables tell us. Using the contemporary unit of distance measurement called a parsec, equal to 3.26 light years, Table 8-4 offers the third proof very clearly.

Star Designation	Parsecs	Light-years	(Usual Listing)
alpha Draconis	87-95	285-310	(300)
alpha Ursae Minoris	185-340	600-1100	(700)
gamma Cephei	15	50	(50)
alpha Cygni	200-490	650-1600	(1000)
alpha Lyrae	8.13	26.5	(26.5)

Table 8-4. Modern Star Distance Best Estimate.

Obviously, the designer wanted to impress the magnitude of this discovery upon the mind of the initiate. Even today, stellar distances simply are not that well known and uncertainty of the estimated measurement increases decidedly faster than the growth in relative value. The designer, however, had confidence in his knowledge and makes a positive statement thereof. With his favorite reiterative teaching technique, he not only points to a particular star, but then unmistakably describes the particular star. The speed of light was known when the Great Pyramid was conceived!

Now cast your newly found insight upon the Grand Gallery and behold the Hall of Light. No more are you fumbling in the darkness of assumption concerning the Great Pyramid unit of measurement. Nor are you further required to haltingly grope in the dim, smoky torchlight of gross ignorance. As you are brought to light, so is the Hall of Light, and you see before you a long-known friend, ROY G BIV: Yes, the seven corbelled levels spell out the seven colors of the rainbow spectrum of visible light—red, orange, yellow, green, blue, indigo and violet.

"A most impressive display, this light seeming to emanate from the very walls without any obvious source," you think to yourself. "I see the light, but I do not have to believe it." Ah, so, initiate, the designer foresaw your hesitation and will confirm your initiation into the fraternity of true believers only after you have stepped through the "e" passage.

IX. CONFIRMATION CENTER

The Antechamber immediately follows the "e" passage. Actually, it will be found to be akin to an interruption of the total "e" passage, since the longer portion of this passage lies ahead beyond this transitional chamber. The nature of this appellation will become obvious to the initiate as the chamber is explained. For now, it is sufficient to note that this place retains the "e" passage basic width, but provides more headroom, except for the area beneath the semi-wall crossing the chamber shortly after the entrance. More will be said about this feature after the chamber itself has been identified.

Referring back to the "e" passage, you remember its central axis is horizontal. The initial portion is defined first by the junction of this axis and the sloping central axis of the "pi" passage and second by the junction of this axis and the sloping extension of the floor line of the "pi" passage. Without the Antechamber interruption, the second junction would lack physical definition. Thus, the Antechamber portion of the "e" passage arises to clearly point out this transition from slope to mid-air horizontal line of thought. So transition really began with the definition of the length of the initial portion of the "e" passage. This is its purpose and the north wall of the chamber so states this fact: The passage does not end at this point, but the secondary portion begins. The continuation of the passage floor level and basic width through the chamber and beyond reinforces this statement.

Definition of the secondary portion, or Antechamber, is that portion of the basic "e" passage where the floor-to-ceiling height has changed from the square root of "e" to six units (148 63/64 inches or 3784.28 mm). This height is the re-use of the word six previously encountered in the Hall of Light and also the product of 1.5 times four.

The length of this chamber of 4.666332184 units (115 7/8 inches or 2943.12 mm) offers no immediate clue to its message. Adding this to the previously identified lengths of this horizontal level provides no further resolution either. In fact, two facts become more clear. The previous lengths belong to the geometric measurement conversion from slope to horizontal "e" passage central axis, and this axis passes unhindered through the total length of the passage including the antechamber. These statements tell you the antechamber is not part of the main message or its confirmation, but that it provides subsidiary information. It is a parenthetical remark aside from the main flow of thought. With this clarification, you may avoid becoming absorbed by the complexities of the chamber.

Thus, to move through this chamber quickly in pursuit of the central purpose, the initiate should first note the floor. Here again transition is noted at .5227210300 units (12 63/64 inches or 329.69 mm) into the chamber where the floor changes from white limestone to rose granite. The limestone floor length does not ring any bells, but the granite section at 4.143611154 units is identical to the half width of both the Learning Center and the King's Chamber. Since we are now seeking confirmation of the speed of light discovery, it appears the yet-to-be-identified word 8.287222307 is related thereto.

Now looking upward to the mid-level of the Antechamber, the initiate finds further transitional evidence. Above the basic "e" passage height, the north wall is limestone while the other three walls are mostly rose granite. Starting from the north wall, the first impediment encountered is the surface of the boss located on the north side of the granite semi-wall. This distance is .8243606355 units (20 15/32 inches or 519.94 mm), or one half of the square root of e, a word previously encountered. Usually overlooked at this point is the fact that the edges of the semi-wall are at this same distance from the north wall where they are implanted in the east and west walls. This means most of the north surface of the semi-wall was purposely cut deeper than the edges and the boss and is consequently further from the north wall. This difference of .0416647683 units (1 1/32 units or 26.28 mm) places the semi-wall north cut surface at .8660254038 units (21 1/2 inches or 546.21 mm). Here is a new word of significance.

In simple terminology, this word can come from a number of sources such as:

$$\sqrt{.75}$$

$$\sqrt{\frac{1.5}{2}}$$

$$\frac{\sqrt{3}}{2}$$

Sin 60°
Cos 30°

However, it also represents a more complex function directly related to the speed of light as defined by the designer of the Great Pyramid. In brief, the speed of light is a constant and equals the wavelength times the frequency, or $c = \lambda f$. This simple relationship is called a rectangular hyperbola and pictorially (graphically) appears as shown in Fig. 9-1. What it says is when λ goes up, f goes down, and vice versa.

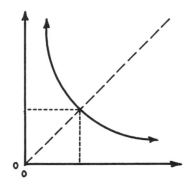

Fig. 9-1. Rectangular Hyperbola Graphic Representation.

The most interesting single point on this curve is its mid-point where λ equals f and the 45° angle line crosses the curve in the graph. This is the line of symmetry and the curve is symmetric one side to the other from this crossing point. Obviously, if c is constant and the two variables equal at this point, then each must equal the square root of c. Or from the designer's point-of-view:

c	$=$	$\underline{1.5} \times 10^{16}$ $=$	15,000,000,000,000,000.
$\sqrt{c}$	$=$	$\sqrt{1.5} \times 10^{8}$ $=$	122,474,487.1
$\sqrt{c}$ Cos 45°	$=$	$\sqrt{1.5/2} \times 10^{8}$ $=$	86,602,540.38
$\sqrt{c}$ Sin 45°	$=$	$\sqrt{1.5/2} \times 10^{8}$ $=$	86,602,540.38

The last two of these represent a single identifying symmetric finger-print value for proving knowledge of the speed of light and the relationship of its component parts. Incidentally, this value is half the distance from the zero point (origin) along the 45° line to the crossing point. If you will recall, the noble relationship used two (or a function thereof) to represent mankind. Thus, this interpretation is speed of light known by mankind.

Leaving the semi-wall north cut surface and progressing to the south face, the initiate again finds the speed-of-light word spoken. The north face distance reference just denoted the components of the speed of light, and when the nominal thickness of the semi-wall of .6339745962 units (15 47/64 inches or 399.86 mm) is added, the next dimension (the south face) says 1.500000000 units from the north wall of the antechamber. This 1.5 is the encoded word for the speed of light, the crux of the message the Great Pyramid speaks to you, the initiate.

Last in this particular series of meaningful distance figures is the next short length of "e" passage width. This length of .1487212710 units (3 11/16 inches or 93.80 mm) plus the prior total of 1.5 equals 1.648721271 units distance, or the square root of e, the same as the passage width. The word "e" has been found to mean either a natural function or use of natural logarithms is close at hand. As it will be revealed, it is the latter, but not quite yet.

Now, a seemingly strange phenomenon takes place. With the remaining 3.017610913 units of distance through the antechamber, the designer has another objective to meet and a combination lesson to teach the initiate. Observe the east and west side walls of this remaining distance. First, you find a pair of recesses, then a space, next another pair of recesses, followed by a space, and finally a third pair of recesses. In all, there are three pairs of recesses symbolizing three drop gate positions and separated by two equal spaces. When measured, each drop gate position is found to be for a gate of .8660254038 units thickness! Here is the wavelength-frequency fin-gerprint redundancy lesson; if the initiate thought the introduction of this word happened to be mere coincidence, this triple repeat must assure him of design intent. The two equal spaces of .2097673505 units (5 13/64 inches or 132.30 mm) each are, of course, separators to distinguish the three gates.

The first part of the combination lesson consisted of re-emphasizing the nature of light. What further enlightenment did the designer wish to bestow? Study this situation carefully, particularly the three symbolic gates. The message is about seeing, the nature of light and the number three. Why, yes, that is the intent—the three primary colors! In light, these are orange, green and violet; combined they produce white light. With the gates up, or open, you and the light may proceed toward fulfillment of confirmation. But suppose all three are lowered and closed. You and the light are completely barred from further advancement. But, you reason, no need for three when one gate could effectively do the job. True, however, the use of the descriptive term "symbolic" has not been taken into account. Accept the gates as representing violet, green and orange filters and you have respectively blocked visible white light.

Mathematics is symbolic facts. So also is the Great Pyramid. Therefore, there is no reason not to accept the three gates as such. This contention is backed up with hard facts, however. Fact one is that no fragment or evidence of actual gates has been found or identified. Fact two is that the antechamber is designed to allow lowering mechanization for the three gates, but this or an easily rebuilt mechanism could be used for raising them, so the common security theory is readily breached. Fact three is that the rose granite side walls of the antechamber arise to differing heights before expanding the width of the topmost portion of the chamber.

The east side wall rises to the same height, 4.143611154 units, as the length of the granite portion of the antechamber floor. Its flat, shelf-like top measures two divided by the wall height or .4826707733 units (11 63/64 inches or 304.43 mm) in width and runs the length of the chamber. From the back of the shelf, the outer wall rises vertically to the ceiling, first as rose granite, then as limestone, with the latter being the same in height as the width of the shelf. Again a reminder of the transitional nature of the antechamber. This band of limestone separates the granite ceiling from all three granite walls; the north wall is all limestone.

Across the antechamber, the west wall differs in that its height is three-quarters of the chamber total, or .75 times 6 equaling 4.5 units (111 47/64 inches or 2838.21 mm). Its higher shelf has the same dimensions as the east shelf, except it has three semi-circular hollows, each centered over a drop-gate position. The bottom of each hollow is level with the east shelf height giving each hollow a radius of .3563888460 units (8 27/32 inches of 224.78 mm), or a diameter less than gate thickness. Thus, the west wall shows the journal boxes necessary for rollers required to lower and raise the indicated gates, but the absence of this same feature on the opposite wall states that this is an area of symbolic movable gates rather than actual ones.

Item	Measurement (Units)	Comments
Floor (Limestone)	.5227210300	
Floor (Rose Granite)	4.143611154	8.287222307 ÷ 2
Floor (Total)	4.666332184	Antechamber Length
N. Wall to Boss	.8243606355	$\sqrt{e} \div 2$
Semi-wall relief	.0416647683	
(Sub-Total)	.8660254038	$\sqrt{.75}$
Semi-wall thickness	.6339745962	
(Sub-Total)	1.500000000	1.5
First Space	.1487212710	
(Sub-Total)	1.648721271	$\sqrt{e}$
First Gate	.8660254038	$\sqrt{.75}$
Second Space	.2097673505	
Second Gate	.8660254038	$\sqrt{.75}$
Third Space	.2097673505	
Third Gate	.8660254038	$\sqrt{.75}$
Total	4.666332184	Antechamber Length
E. Wall Height	4.143611156	8.287222307 ÷ 2
W. Wall Journal Boxes	.3563888460	Radius
W. Wall Height (Sub-Total)	4.500000000	4.5 or .75 × 6
W. Wall Outer Granite	1.017329227	
Limestone Band	.4826707733	4 ÷ 8.287222307
Total Height	6.000000000	6
"e" Passage Width	1.648721271	$\sqrt{e}$ or $e^{.5}$
Semi-Wall & Gates	1.913066325	1 ÷ .5227210300
Upper Chamber Width	2.614062818	$\sqrt{e}+(8\div8.287222307)$

Table 9-1. Primary Dimensions of Antechamber.

Yes, the antechamber is transitional and Table 9-1 shows yet another instance demonstrating design intent. In taking in the overall chamber and particularly the semi-wall, the initiate most likely will miss seeing the side walls starting as limestone but changing to rose granite one unit into the chamber. This happens in the area of the semi-wall but is mostly hidden by its recessed ends. Intent is shown by the next to last Table listing showing that the one unit of initial side wall limestone divided by the initial floor limestone equals the width of the semi-wall and the three gates. This width minus the "e" passage width, with the remainder divided by two, gives the recess dimension of each of these four features as .1321725270 units (3 9/32 inches or 83.36 mm).

Since the initiate is in the final phase of the initiation, the natural inclination to get on with the confirmation will be pursued. The main point of this transitional chamber has been made; that is, a mathematical fingerprint of the speed of light has been found to back up the general statement of the Hall of Light. Further transitional insights can await the review, or reflections upon initiation.

Proceeding to the third and final part of the "e" passage, the initiate finds it the same as the first portion, except for length and material of construction. The Great Pyramid here speaks a single, simple word—four—an even four units (99 21/64 inches or 2522.85 mm), all in rose granite. No more transition, but a word in color. A word related to transition, but beyond it as part of the final confirmation. Just as your initiation began with the word four for the base sides of the pyramid, so shall it conclude with four of something now to be discovered. Actually, both the cross-section of "e" area and the length of four are the clues. The volume of 4e indicates confirmation, as four times a natural function or logarithm is the sought after confirmation.

At last the initiate steps from the "e" passage into the King's Chamber of the Great Pyramid. The fatigue of the journey is felt, but the senses are keyed to a high level. If this chamber speaks as promised, the journey will not have been in vain. The initiate will be relieved to know he has correctly understood the message the Great Pyramid speaks, the genius of the designer impressed upon his mind; and the thrill of discovery of previously unsuspected ancient knowledge will refresh a spirit wearied by transient worries. Step forward now and be confirmed in this large rose granite chamber.

Before you make the 90° turn to the right, observe the north-south width of the King's Chamber. This dimension is identical to that same dimension in the Learning Center at 8.287222307 units (205 25/32 inches or 5226.86 mm). Yes, you have heard this word before but not understood its meaning. It was also found in the ascending "pi" passage girdle stones and in variations in the chamber of transition. Here it is again as part of the confirmation. But wait a minute before jumping to conclusions.

Now, make your right turn and check the east-west length of the King's Chamber. You find this to be exactly twice the width. Remember the designer's mode of operation: Redundant usage of a basic word emphasizes its importance. Here in rose granite, not only is importance emphasized, but significance to confirmation is shouted loud and clear! Oh, you remember hearing this word, yet understanding and meaning need guidance. All right, clue-by-clue, whence came you?

— Entrance offset: Summer solstice (standstill) as number of days with *sun*set within one *minute* of time.
— Descending "pi" passage: Points to north *star*.
— Ascending "pi" passage: Points toward a *south*erly *elevation*.
— Total "pi" passages: *Speed of light measurement of star distance.*
— King's Chamber: *Largest, highest* chamber constructed of rose (*reddish* colored) granite.

"The mean (average) light distance from the surface of the sun to the surface of the earth is 8.287222307 minutes!" declares the Great Pyramid. This converts to 236,350,652,700 units, 92,627,373 miles, or 149,069,589 kilometers. When using light as a basis, the surface-to-surface distance makes sense because visible sunlight must leave from the sun's surface and human observers most likely are on the surface of the earth. Many modern reference sources use "about 8 1/3 minutes" based on the usual center-to-center distance. Reference sources do vary, usually due to frequent remeasurement, but deducting the average sun and earth radii from the center-to-center average distance gives the Great Pyramid an excellent accuracy rating by today's standards. Here then is the first confirmation from the King's Chamber, and the second from the half area level, that the designer indeed knew of and caused the Great Pyramid to speak in terms of the speed of light.

Length and width have spoken in unison to reveal their part in this confirmation, so what does the height of the King's Chamber have to say? You quickly note its measurement of 9.210340372 units (228 45/64 inches or 5809.09 mm); moments later you realize this is equal to the natural logarithm of ten thousand, or $\ln 10^4$, or $\ln \sqrt[4]{10^{16}}$. Can this refer to the 1.5×10^{16} units per year speed of light? And what about the final portion of the "e" passage referring to e, or $\ln$, and four? Is there some way to back up this connection? But, of course, visualize the extension of the floor line of the Hall of Light as shown in Fig. 9-2 and you have the connection perfectly.

Geometrically, the designer has completed the visible construction within the Great Pyramid as can be seen by the upper left corner of the King's Chamber in Fig. 9-2, Cross-Section of the Half-Area Level. In so doing, he scored another point for confirmation in relating the final chamber height to the speed of light. So, is that it? No one final resounding confirmation to clinch the case? Do not underestimate the designer, initiate, for you are not yet confirmed as a believer.

Behold that which stands free before you—the open coffer. What do you see in this empty, lid-less chest? The initiate stands dumbfounded; someone forgot something! Again the question is asked. This time the initiate says, "Nothing." The third time the question is asked, the initiate sees the light: The designer put the answer into the container itself. Here then is the final confirmation. What does this slightly discolored, single block of hollowed-out rose granite have to say?

Coffer Dimension	Units	Inches	Millimeters
(L) Outside Length	3.609593890	89 5/8	2276.62
(W) Outside Width	1.550561685	38 1/2	977.96
(H) Outside Height	1.663726349	41 5/16	1049.33
(l) Inside Length	3.135253416	77 55/64	1977.45
(w) Inside Width	1.072983013	26 41/64	676.75
(h) Inside Height	1.383992683	34 23/64	872.90
End Wall Thickness	.2371702370	5 57/64	149.59
Side Wall Thickness	.2387893360	5 59/64	150.61
Bottom Thickness	.2797336660	6 15/16	176.43

Table 9-2. Design Dimensions of the Coffer.

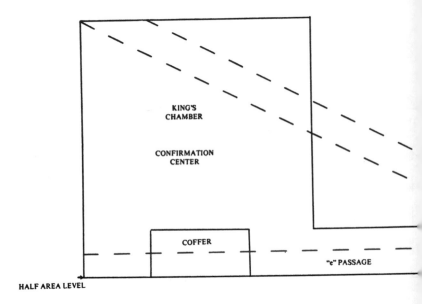

Fig. 9-2: Cross-Section of the Half-Area Level.

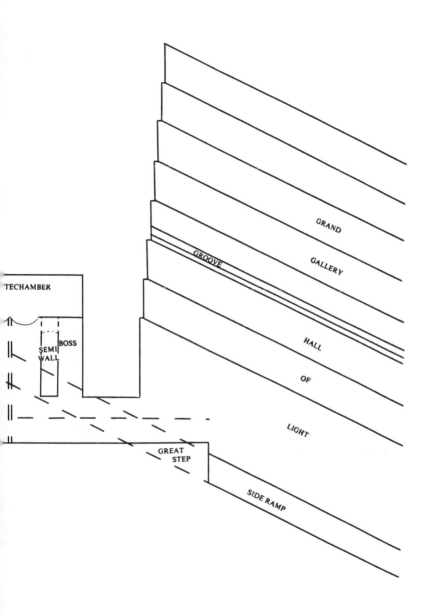

Since the coffer is undecorated and unadorned, the initiate realizes that it, as the Great Pyramid has demonstrated, must speak with the language of dimensional analysis. As he checks the coffer's measurements, the initiate remembers the significance of the east-west central cross-section of the pyramid being central to teaching the truth of ancient knowledge of the speed of light. Here again he is on a central cross-section of the pyramid, but this time it is the north-south axis, and here is the only place within the pyramid that this can occur. Perhaps this coordinate defines confirmation message significance.

The most obvious relationship found concerns the outside volume (LWH) at 9.311706650 cubic units and the inside volume (lwh) at 4.655853325 cubic units. You immediately discern the former is twice, or two times, the latter. Here is a direct reference to the word "man" in the noble relationship. Alternatively, you can turn this around and say the inside volume, or empty space, is one half of the outside, or total, volume. This ingenious design thus states that the volume of the empty space is exactly equal to the volume of the coffer's solid shell of granite. So far you have two clues to verify design intent. Go on.

That the Great Pyramid is symbolic should be recalled to your mind at this time. So too is the coffer both in content and in confirmation. In this case it could hold water, both literally and figuratively. Naturally, your impulse is to ask how should you know this to be true. The designer anticipated your question and intentionally put the answer before you as an empty stone container, made from a single block of very carefully selected specific stone. You realize the symbolic content had to be water, with a specific gravity of unity (1, even), when you discover the specific gravity of the coffer granite is 2.718281828 (e, even), by design intent!

However pleasing this third coffer confirmation clue is to the initiate, he must realize the whole interior of the Great Pyramid has had continuity of message theme built around the word "e". This clue, though, is a straight, simple reference to "e" itself rather than a variant thereof. Vexed by the coffer's dimensions, which do not reveal an immediate explanation by inspection, the initiate is reminded of the Niche. The lesson learned there was the progression from "e" to exponents to natural logarithms. This suggested solution, learned there, will apply here. The question is how.

After attempting a number of applications which do not apply, the initiate begins to awaken to interrelationships among the Table 9-2 figures. His list begins to grow, and of course some initial equalities prove otherwise, causing their elimination from further consideration. This matching game continues until the initiate is convinced he is on the right track to final, positive confirmation. Using the prior table abbreviations of capital letters for outside dimensions and lower case letters for inside dimensions, a short table of simple relationships appears as follows:

Relationship	Value in Units
$LWH = 2 \ lwh$	9.311706650
$LH = lh^2$	6.005376464
$LW = Hlw$	5.596897984
$L = lw^2$	3.609593890
$H = Ww$	1.663726349
$H^2 = 2h$	2.767985364
$W^2H = 4$	4.000000000
$Wh = 2w = H^{1.5}$	2.145966026
$Hh = \ln 10$	2.302585093

Table 9-3. Some of the Coffer Dimensional Relationships.

The code of the coffer is cracking. Table 9-3 is sufficient to show five important insights:

1. The use of the natural logarithm of ten, two identified words.
2. An exponential use of the key word 1.5, or speed-of-light reference.
3. An even four, which the final portion of the "e" passage fingered.
4. Width and height dimensions are closely interrelated.
5. The length dimensions only appear as a pair.

Very quickly the initiate resolves the width and height equivalencies question. These are:

$$w = 1.072983013 = \sqrt{\frac{\ln 10}{2}} = \frac{\sqrt{2 \ln 10}}{2} = \frac{H}{W}$$

$$H = 1.663726349 = \sqrt[3]{2 \ln 10} = \frac{4}{W^2} = Ww$$

$$h = 1.383992683 = \sqrt[3]{\frac{(\ln 10)^2}{2}} = \frac{\ln 10}{H}$$

$$W = 1.550561685 = \sqrt[6]{\frac{2^5}{\ln 10}} = \frac{2}{\sqrt{H}}$$

Length dimensions are more puzzling. The inside length of the coffer is dependent upon the outside length dimension. That much is clear. Proceeding from the widths and heights you can find the ratio of (L) to (1), and even find an introduction to common logarithms to the base 10, but the basis of L does not yield yet.

$$(1) = 3.135253416 = (2)(\log e^L) = \frac{2L}{\ln 10} = \frac{L}{w^2}$$

Now the initiate is becoming anxious. He knows which of the coffer's dimensions is the key to final, positive confirmation, but not what it represents. The designer has slipped in a last laugh to remind the initiate of humility in his moment of triumphant entry into the fraternity of truth and knowledge.

$$L = 3.609593890 = (\ln 10)(\log e^L) = \ln 10^{L/\ln 10}$$

$$= \frac{Password}{4\sqrt[6]{2^7} \ln 10} = \frac{Password}{2^3 \sqrt{H}}$$

What is the password? Obviously, it is 37.24682660, but what does it represent? As the question is repeated, "What is the password?", the initiate ponders the possibilities in his mind. He knows he knows the proper answer, but hesitates, because he is not yet convinced he is right. One more moment to review the clues of the coffer. Ah, the light is dawning: Four times the product of the outside dimensions of the coffer equals the password.

$$4\,LWH = Password$$

In a flash, the initiate knows the answer. He has convinced himself, as the designer intended all along, that mankind once knew with certainty the speed of light and all that may be inferred therefrom. In the unseen presence of the master architect himself, as the Great Pyramid speaks to you, the latest initiate, for the third and final time, "What is the password?" Without fear or hesitation you reply, "The natural logarithm of 1.5×10^{16}."

A seemingly long pause follows. You know you have successfully found the path your ancient ancestors wanted you to find for yourself. They left the Great Pyramid as a trailmarker. You heeded its silent shout and understood the message it had to speak. As you stand in silent awe at the startling impact of its message, you hear the four closing words of your now accomplished initiation:

So may it be.

PART TWO

REFLECTIONS

X. INTERPRETATION

Reflecting upon the just-completed initiation, the newly-initiated realizes a significant event has occurred in his life but remains unsure of the impact of the initiation in his own mind. Therefore, a review is in order to clarify unclear points and impress meaningful interpretation by emphasizing and expanding orderly comprehension and progression. Some of you at this point will see clearly and understand the continuity and meaning of those things the Great Pyramid has spoken to you during initiation. The majority of initiates will with reservation agree it spoke, but reserve judgment on whether it was to each personally or meaningfully. And, of course, the skeptics will remain as a vocal minority unsure that the Great Pyramid Speaks to You, in any way.

For nine chapters, I have been your escort and guide to follow the designer's train of thought. It is one thing to promulgate one's own thoughts, and yet another to direct your attention to another's message. Initially, the Great Pyramid of Giza drew your attention itself, or you would not be here. The largest and best constructed of all pyramids presented a mystery and a challenge. Why? The human intellect does not accept an enduring enigma; it wants explanation in acceptable, rational terminology. One way to do this is to propose an acceptable explanation, then provide research to support the contention. Unfortunately, judicious selection may overlook the real truth of the matter or message. More difficult to allow and achieve is freedom of complete continuity necessary for truth to speak for itself, and be so accepted, in spite of individual preconceptions or bias.

What is the truth, if the Great Pyramid is allowed to speak of and for itself? That it draws you to it is a promise. Can you then be satisfied to let your preconceptions or bias prevent it from speaking to you? Why would so vast a design and masterpiece of craftsmanship be executed as an enduring enigma? To so believe becomes a discordant conclusion lodged in one's inner memory. The only logical way out of this dilemma then is to let it speak to you for itself. And if it is to speak to you, it had to be designed to do so—to teach you its vocabulary in terms you would understand.

The starting point, after attaining your attention, is common sense. If I want to tell you something, I must get your attention, use a common language in a progression of terms that make sense, and if you are to believe your ears and my message, order it in a logical, self-proving presentation. Your initiation began on the basis of a triad of assumptions that had to self-prove ("hold water") to be believable. First was the assumption that if the Great Pyramid did carry a hidden message, it must be in the universal language of mathematics. Second, if the message is significant, it must be important for the pyramid to provide the key itself for decoding its own message. And third, each and every significant detail must confirm and contribute to the reading of the message and establishing its validity.

Now you will ask why the designer should have taken such painstaking care to get you to make these assumptions. For one simple, obvious reason: It would be difficult enough for you to believe his knowledge and awe-inspiring genius. Thus, to convince you of design intent and message content, he had to override your initial individual persuasions and invoke your trust in the impartial guide called logic.

Continuing your initiation, the key for proving the initial assumptions was found to be the exterior dimensions of the pyramid itself. Shall we say the first solid clue to solving the mystery is so obvious as to be easily overlooked, and yet it is logically located. The point of Chapter II is determination of the Great Pyramid standard Unit of measurement. Determining a unit by use of the exact solar year is not new, since the Unit I had you use in subsequent chapters is included in the range of values deduced by Isaac Newton. What is new is the use of the previously unexplained very slight skew of the pyramid sides to tentatively verify the standard Unit.

As I noted in the Foreword, numerous reference sources were drawn upon. In referring to the exterior or casing stone blocks, several sources noted the material as polished white limestone which becomes harder as it ages. Since the surfaces of the few remaining blocks are nowhere described as inscribed with hieroglyphs or other symbols existent today, the stones of the Great Pyramid must speak in concert, if at all. Other pyramids and other reports to the contrary, embellishments (even if original) would detract from, rather than add to, an encoded message. In other words, why write it, or inscribe it, if you can just show a message in simple geometric lines?

Now with a tentative standard Unit, you become anxious to test it for confirmation. This test proves out in the third chapter and provides a heightened degree of confidence in both the approach and assumptions. Some major clues are beginning to fall into an orderly progression. Should this continue, respect and awe for the designer's ingenuity compound geometrically. At this point, however, a single confirmation raises hope, but must not cause you to jump to conclusions.

Although not noted in the initiation, it might be well to now observe the shape of a pyramid and its relation to the idea of a series in mathematics. I am certain that if the mantle of the Great Pyramid were still in place it would reflect more light on this subject and several others, including the core masonry evidence of apparent parabolic dishing of each side. Be that as it may, the series countdown is of interest here as a concept and later as implemented in several ways.

A simple pictorial series,

——	Row 1
—— ——	Row 2
—— —— ——	Row 3
—— —— —— ——	Row 4
—— —— —— —— ——	Row 5
	Etc. to n

leads to some interesting mathematical curios:

Two Dimensional		Three Dimensional	
n	Σn	n^2	Σn^2
1 (2^0)	1	1 (2^0)	1
2 (2^1)	3	4 (2^2)	5
3	6	9	14

Two Dimensional		Three Dimensional	
4 (2^2)	10	16 (2^4)	30
5	15	25	55
6	21	36	91
7	28	49	140
8 (2^3)	36	64 (2^6)	204
9	45	81	285
10	55	100	385
11	66	121	406
12	78	144	650
.	.	.	.
.	.	.	.
.	.	.	.
n	($\frac{1}{2}$) (n) (n + 1)	(2Σn) $-$ n	$\dfrac{(2n)(2n+1)(n+1)}{12}$
.	.	.	.
.	.	.	.
.	.	.	.
200	20,100	40,000	2,686,700
201	21,301	40,401	2,727,101

The reason I show the n = 200 and 201 rows is because several sources indicate the number of rows in the original Great Pyramid to be one or the other. Thus, a perfect and solid structure would have used the total number of blocks indicated. Owing to the raised central bedrock base and the various passages and chambers, the common estimate of approximately 2,300,000 actual blocks used seems reasonable. Besides the reference check, however, the example illustrates how simple numbers and relationships may be combined to produce simple, precise information without resorting to complicated rules and formulas.

Proceeding step by logical step, the meaning of the noble relationship is exemplified in the fourth chapter. Noble in that mathematically a valid equation designed in stone relates the rational to the transcendental. But why confound simple mathematics with the philosophical, you may ask. Just remember, the former is as the language to transmit the latter. It is saying, "As man the integer is to the aggregate earth, so is this pyramid to the universe." In addition, it confirms that by seeking after known constants you too shall be enlightened by further precise relationships.

Surely, your mind will question the noble relationship on one count. And that is that the designer ignored God in this relationship. Not so, if you think as he did: Let God be represented by unity or one, and you will find Him everywhere, in the universal language of mathematics. Unobtrusive, but there; and if you doubt the indivisibility of this unity, check its reciprocal, powers and roots. Furthermore, consider this reference in relation to the concept of monotheism, or one God. Roughly fifteen hundred years after the presumed construction date of the Great Pyramid, Amenhotep IV (eighteenth dynasty) temporarily established this doctrine and simultaneously changed his name to Chuen'eten. However, shortly after his passing, his unity reformation was quickly laid to rest. Some other sources state his name change was to Akhnaton (Ikhnaton), with his reign listed as c. 1379-1362 B.C., and best remembered as the husband of the renowned Nefertiti. His second son-in-law, Tutankhaton, changed his own name to the now famous Tutankhamen (King Tut).

Since numerous ancient Egyptian names such as Hu (Huni), Khufu, Isesi, and Khui, to name just a few, have a definite Far East association, I tried an experiment with Chuen'eten. I wrote just his name on pieces of paper and gave each separately to persons knowledgeable in Oriental etymology. Each was asked only to try to identify the word and its background by inspection alone—no research. Surprisingly enough this informal approach came up unanimously as ancient Chinese. One source went so far as to say it translates as "Complete Eden" and most likely came from the Yaan area of Szechwan Province by or before 1200 B.C. In checking this out, I learned this area straddles 30° N. latitude and is on the very old trail leading west through Lhasa, Tibet, also almost on the same latitude as the Great Pyramid. Coincidence? Maybe, but then again...

Actually, the subject of the noble relationship is neither an exercise nor a stopping place for endless philosophical debate. It is but a step along the trail of logic to that which you seek, a greater knowledge of the heritage of man. Or more pointedly, you want only to know enough of how it is said to know what the message means.

To get on with the business at hand, Chapter V has you armed with the theory of decoding the message mystery of the Great Pyramid and diligently looking for a logical ingress sequence. As if to confirm and validate theory, an approach along the designer's line of thought proves to fit the source facts. At this point the theory is starting to jell as truth. Should successive successes substantiate such a sliver of satisfaction, surely solution by self-proof shall stand solid and sound.

But why, you may ask, did the designer use the latest sunset rounded to the nearest minute, rather than the earth's aphelion (furthest distance from the sun) on the 14th day after the longest day of the year, or why not the earliest sunrise on any number of other days? The answer, of course, is he knew that what he used precisely related the exterior and interior design plans using the same unit of measurement. Let me clarify this point in tabular form using 1977 Chicago, Illinois, data:

Local Data for Chicago, Illinois, for 1977 (CDT)

Date	Sunrise (AM)	Sunset (PM)	Day Time	Comment
June 1	5:18	8:19	15:01	
2	5:18	8:19	15:01	
3	5:18	8:20	15:02	
4	5:17	8:21	15:04	
5	5:17	8:21	15:04	
6	5:17	8:22	15:05	
7	5:17	8:23	15:06	
8	5:16	8:23	15:07	
9	5:16	8:24	15:08	
10	5:16	8:24	15:08	
11	5:15*	8:25	15:10	
12	5:15*	8:25	15:10	
13	5:15*	8:26	15:11	
14	5:15*	8:26	15:11	
15	5:15*	8:27	15:12	*Earliest Sunrises
16	5:15*	8:27	15:12	
17	5:15*	8:27	15:12	
18	5:15*	8:28	15:13	
19	5:15*	8:28	15:13	
20	5:16	8:28	15:12	
21	5:16	8:29**	15:13	Solstice 7:14 (AM)
22	5:16	8:29**	15:13	
23	5:16	8:29**	15:13	
24	5:16	8:29**	15:13	

Date	Sunrise (AM)	Sunset (PM)	Day Time	Comment
June 25	5:17	8:29**	15:12	
26	5:17	8:29**	15:12	
27	5:18	8:29**	15:11	**Latest Sunsets
28	5:18	8:29**	15:11	
29	5:18	8:29**	15:11	
30	5:19	8:29**	15:10	
July 1	5:19	8:29**	15:10	
2	5:20	8:29**	15:09	
3	5:20	8:29**	15:09	
4	5:21	8:28	15:07	
5	5:22	8:28	15:06	Aphelion
6	5:22	8:28	15:06	
7	5:23	8:27	15:04	
8	5:23	8:27	15:04	
9	5:24	8:27	15:03	
10	5:25	8:26	15:01	

Rounding to the nearest minute accounts for the slight aberrations shown, such as the total day time on June 20th. However, the interesting point is how well the designer knew this equation of time 4500 years or more ago. Even more interesting is the fact of the daily subdivisions we call minutes. This is surprising because current reference sources claim it was the Sumerians, along about 2000 B.C., who first came up with a plan for dividing the day into hours. Perhaps, they too, as the ancient Greeks freely admitted to doing, roamed the known world picking up bits and pieces of former knowledge and receiving the credit therefor. Whether you would label them great plagiarists or great preservers of what they found is a matter of viewpoint. I prefer the latter term, for without their preservation and dissemination of these tidbits, we would not be where we are today.

Both this step and the next step of the initiation (sixth chapter) call attention to the North pole star. Too often, what one sees is assumed to be what another saw. Our present "fixed" star, or North Star, is alpha Ursae Minoris (Pólaris) thanks to the Earth's very slow wobble. Presuming the designer committed his knowledge to stone about 4500 years ago, the then North Star was alpha Draconis (Thuban), an entirely different star. Most likely, however, the interred knowledge is of greater age than the Great Pyramid itself, but the difference in pole stars must be remembered as important to what the message is trying to say to you.

Chapter VI continues the use of the Great Pyramid unit as the validation of theory proceeds. Both descending and ascending passages read out as "pi" passages in cross-sectional area. The universal constant confirms proper decoding. Following this, the "phi" proportion is introduced. Again, the Greeks are generally given credit for the discovery of this "perfect" proportion, which incidentally has been discovered as a natural function several times, including the Fibonacci series. However, the designer is not going to dwell on phi, but demonstrates a function of this number to denote how he folded or proportioned the two parts of the "pi" passage. The point to focus on is the almost 311.5 total length number, even though the ascending portion was originally hidden.

Another number introduced is one and a half. It is not further identified at this step but is re-used again and again in succeeding steps. You could say it is another stepping-stone clue to proper solution of the mystery of design intent.

What is apparent is that, in its original finished condition, a person accidentally finding access would find inside only the descending "pi" passage, pit passage and unfinished pit chamber. Without having insight into design intent, the finder would reasonably assume he had discovered a grandiose, but uncompleted tomb. Presumably then, he would write this off as a "dry" well and proceed elsewhere since the clues we are following have been so obvious as to be overlooked.

Once the hidden or upper interior design is attained, the sequence of clues marches on to become more enlightening and intriguing. Every specific detail falls precisely in place to impress upon your mind that this pyramid was designed to speak to you of things once known. In the seventh step, the Great Pyramid explains how precise calculations may be accomplished. It actually confirms the message theory as indeed intended and does so with such a delicate sense of humor, you must be convinced the designer so thoroughly knew of what he spoke to be able to so jest with his audience.

The Queen's Chamber and stepped passage are indeed the learning center, the place to consolidate your theory and clues, so you may believe the message about to be given to you on this, your first real initiation into what was. First, you learned of the "three" passage from its cross-sectional area. This abruptly converted into the "four and a half" passage providing you with not only the 1.5 number confirmation, but also the learning center ratio. Along with its reciprocal, the ratio carried over to the chamber design for emphasis.

Then you were presented with the three-dimensional puzzle called the Niche. Here at last was a challenge and opportunity to exercise the rationale the designer had been teaching you as part of his message. Solve this and you verify one of the ancient secrets of which this pyramid was designed to speak.

"Impossible," you say as you work your way up through the puzzle. "Certainly you jest with me for we all have been taught that natural logarithms to the base 'e' were first published in 1614 by John Napier, a Scotsman, 4200 years later."

"Sorry," the Niche replies, "I, the designer, knew and used them long ago. In fact, you have been traversing the square root of 'e,' the base of the hyperbolic logarithm system, as the width of each passage all the way from the entrance to this place."

Perhaps, instead of saying the designer used the Niche as a jest, it would be more appropriate to call it a teaser. Of course, there are a number of possibilities for leading an initiate from fractional numbers to exponents to logarithms, but the method used, an ingenious puzzle, is perfectly designed to stimulate and satisfy curiosity step-by-step. This recess, so often barely noted, converts conjecture and theory into precise mathematical proof of design intent and confirms that the Great Pyramid does indeed speak to you of ancient wonders of advanced knowledge. Starting from the simple ten times the reciprocal of the Learning Center ratio, it progresses to e and powers thereof, to functions of the previously identified numbers of 1.5 and 2, to a combination of these and e, and finally to the demonstration not just of the knowledge of e alone, but of e as the base of the system of natural logarithms. Here then is the visual proof of the power of speech saying, "Believe me, not only were precise multidecimal numbers used, but also note that advanced complex calculations were simplified by the use of logarithms."

If this stirring message is not enough to make you sit up and take notice, you may wish to take notice of the pyramid of Sahure's queen at Abusir, which has been recorded as having an e proportion. I do not have the actual data handy for verification, but you may wish to check on half of the base perimeter divided by the height, or depth, as the initiation points out to be the correct interpretation. This suggestion is meant to call your attention to the fact, if present pyramid sequencing is correct, that this pyramid is apparently more than one person's lifetime newer, or more recent, than the Great Pyramid. This could be just a continuation of the knowledge of the value of the e rather than application thereof. This bit of other e magnitude evidence is not alone, however.

More or less contemporary to the Great Pyramid's presumed conception, a strange coincidence was taking place. Across western and northern Europe for over a thousand miles, megalithic man was erecting mysterious mounds, standing stones, structures such as Stonehenge and many others, all based on a common unit of measurement, the megalithic yard. This alone is interesting in that it was spread across a time span of centuries, but the magnitude of the megalithic yard is an astonishing 2.72, not 3, feet (remember, e = 2.718$^+$). The foot is an old unit of measurement, and maybe it has changed over the centuries it has been in use. Or, has it? Strangely enough, the evidence of the common 2.72 yard is beginning to firm up in the new world also. Why? It is not the Great Pyramid Unit, but possibly some itinerant architect did not progress far enough in his initiation.

This remarkable chapter concluded with the open question concerning the importance of 1.5 as the base of a system yet to be determined: So far this, or a variation thereof, has been a reiterated figure indicating importance not yet made clear. Besides the square root and 1.5 itself, you have seen it tied to e and as 15, or 1.5 times ten to the first power. As you were leaving the Learning Center, the volume of the "three" passage again impressed this value upon your memory, but this time as 150, (3 × 50), or as intended, 1.5 times ten to the second power. As you can see, the whole message has more to say and is leading up to a climax. To this point, it has been impressive mathematically with a promise of greater significance to come.

As Chapter VIII opens, you were standing at the lower end of the Grand Gallery, or Hall of Light. This largest single constructed cavity yet discovered in any pyramid dwarfs the observer. Its lines of perspective make one feel small, almost insignificant; and yet it is uplifting to behold and ascend. Even though its height is finite, the imparted feeling is that of transcending the limits of visual perception. Being so-prepared, you, the initiate, are ready to continue your quest for more of the message and meaning of which the Great Pyramid speaks so eloquently.

At first, and in rapid succession, come additional mathematical truths. Just as the design partially converts, to integrate both sloping and vertical lines, so too in vertical cross-section does the designer introduce new concepts of zero, positive and negative numbers, and a summation series with limits. The last of these was noted as useful in the introduction of elementary concepts for teaching integral calculus. Possibly, at this point you might question the designer's methods and wish for a fast, stunning revelation. But observe his method carefully; instead of cryptological tables and formulas which were impractical for his purpose, he simply steps logically through concepts, none of which taken out of context would rate a second thought. Taken as intended, however, conceptual synergism is achieved. That is, when taken together, a greater impact is imparted than when taken individually. You see, the designer was not trying to teach a course in mathematics as such, but rather demonstrate convincingly his knowledge of the truth which the Great Pyramid is about to speak to you.

As you ascended the Grand Gallery you noticed three things: the 27 pairs of side ramp holes with their wall blocks and cross-slashes, the 36 ceiling blocks each notched into the top of the side walls, and the full-length pair of grooves in the lower portion of the fifth level (third corbel). Individually, these did not mean much until you inverted the situation, much as you converted height to depth as a concept, and realized the designer has the Great Pyramid speaking to you about a great big, long 1.5 word. He used the whole Grand Gallery as an enormous billboard to try to get his message across to you.

After arriving at the Great Step and finding its pair of corner holes and briefly studying the first portion of the "e" passage, the initiate remains puzzled. Why all the advertising along his route, then the sudden feeling that he had missed the point? The first portion of the "e" passage provides the missing clue for it is geometrically designed to teach raising one's sights to the mid-point or central axis level of the passage. Now the initiate is prepared to see the clue that so many others have missed.

Imbedded in the central lip of the Great Step is a valley, ignored previously as the usual erosion caused by countless feet scuffing over the edge. This is a strange preconception when no other floor area shows anywhere near a like amount of wear. With the realization that much of the erosion had to have been a designed incision, inspiration fills the gap. As you had wished at the beginning of the Grand Gallery, all the clues suddenly fall into place for a swift, stunning revelation: The designer knew the speed of light. The overlooked valley in the Great Step had done its job as a symbolic beam-splitter. Figuratively, it stopped your preconceptions dead on the east-west central axis of the pyramid (step riser) and allowed the light of logic to proceed.

Gazing back along the lengths of the Grand Gallery you are still trying to recover from the shock of learning that the central point of the message the Great Pyramid speaks is an extremely accurate report on the speed of light. The beam-splitter gave it away, but the listing in the eighth chapter shows the gallery billboard in total spelled out 1.5×10^{16} units for this universal constant. You see your shock stemming from the fact that almost any person today casually speaks about the speed of light, even though hard pressed to give even an approximate figure in current measurement systems, whereas no one really thought their ancient ancestors could have such knowledge. And not only knew thereof, but used a simple system of measurement based thereon to communicate this fact to us. The most remarkable achievement you are ever apt to discover has just been revealed too quickly to be fully absorbed and accepted.

In recognition of your dilemma, the designer immediately verifies your conclusion with a statement of his beliefs and knowledge. He has had the Great Pyramid point to the North polar star position and say 311.5 light-years distance. At this point you could still say it is possible that any star at that particular distance might be a candidate. In fact, if the designer or others had come from beyond our solar system itself, this would be an indirect way of indicating the neighborhood in which to look, if indeed the old homestead still existed. But let us look at the evidence.

A little over a century ago, Piazzi Smyth determined that the Great Pyramid was laid out when alpha Draconis was the pole star between 3440 and 2123 B.C., and this period includes the Golden Age of Egyptian pyramid construction. By today's best astronomic measurement, the designer's 311.5 light-year measurement confirms alpha Draconis as the only pole star to fit the fact. Only if none of the cycle of precession pole stars had fit, would it make sense to indicate "a star," then give an address outside of this particular circle of candidates.

By the way, notice that the designer states a hard fact as 311.4883214 light years. The best modern equivalent is 300, perhaps 310, light-years, and at this distance uncertainties of 50%, or even 100%, are not uncommon. So, accepting the designer's fact and putting a ± 5% tolerance on it (by modern standards this is wildly optimistic on the tight side, I am told), you find 245 known stars currently within these limits. The point being made here is that the present state-of-the-art of astronomy tends to confirm, but cannot disprove, the logic of the alpha Draconis identification. The Great Pyramid not only points directly to where it was at approximately the right time, but it also states its precise address, which is well within the neighborhood we now tentatively know. This correlation, along with the designer's consistent use of simple, straightforward logic and fact, attests with renewed certainty to the time of this pyramid's construction, the extent of the designer's knowledge, and the accuracy of his facts and system of measurement. Incidentally, the late Dr. Albert Einstein proposed that a new, accurate system of measurement could be constructed using the diameter and mass of the hydrogen atom and the speed of light as the base units.

Since we are speaking of accuracy, you should not have been too surprised at the initiation reference to use of a laser. Symbolically used, of course, to illuminate the beam-splitter, but accurate enough to also allow the boring and setting of square-edged passages as straight as a beam of light. In addition, the laser and beam-splitter concepts are indicative of knowledge concerning holography, the production of holograms recording two patterns of light from a single source of coherent light. These in turn may be reconstructed as mid-air, three-dimensional pictures capable of presenting differing perspectives as you move around them. Indeed, just as a laser has its constructive uses, so also could one have been misused to initiate the destructive erosion of the Great Step valley. As you stand on the brink of the Great Step viewing the Grand Gallery which has now become the Hall of Light, you see the seven colors of the rainbow in the seven corbels and realize lasers can produce all of these plus more than meets the eye.

As the ninth chapter opened you had seen the light and were preparing to confirm your findings starting with the Antechamber, or chamber of transition. This second portion of the "e" passage dimensionally varied only in height from the first and third portions. However, it introduced the conversion of construction stone from white limestone to rose granite and consisted of a series of conversions. Just as these two changes signified, the designer's line of thought changed also: The geometric trail which led to the discovery of the Great Pyramid message speaking of the speed of light converts to a trail of confirming evidence that you heard the message correctly.

The chamber floor first reminds the initiate of the 8.287222307 word not yet translated. Later, the east wall and both east and west wall shelves do likewise. But the confirmation line of thought really takes off from the face of the north wall at mid-chamber height.

First, solid confirmation evidence is found immediately in initial chamber length dimensions. Here, the designer provides the proof that he not only knew the speed of light as a universal constant, but also that he knew of its two components, wavelength and frequency. He produces the significant fingerprint to back up the spoken word of the Great Pyramid. Measuring from the limestone north wall to the raised boss on the granite semi-wall you found the square root of "e" divided by two, or a word related to the Hall of Light. From the north wall to the north nominal face of the semi-wall you found the square root of one half of 1.5, or the fingerprint clue for the two component variables of the constant speed of light. Again, from the north chamber wall, this time to the south face of the semi-wall, you discovered the word 1.5 meaning "speed of light." And finally from the same north wall to the edge of the first gate recess, you identified the square root of e word itself signifying the return to the significant passages' common width. This part of the message is heard as, "The revelation of the *Hall of Light* consists of *two components* equaling the *speed of light* leading to the sloping *passages* precisely measuring usage and horizontal *passages* each leading to further instruction."

Since the designer changes his focus of attention at this point, I will take a minute to throw a little light on the semi-wall boss just mentioned. I spoke of it briefly early in the initiation long before we arrived at its location. It has been badly defaced and mutilated. This semi-conic section, level with the initial north face surface of the semi-wall, has engendered an enormous amount of speculation due to its particular shape.

Fig. 10-1. The Shape of the Semi-Wall Boss.

Other lifting bosses remain on some of the building stones of the Great Pyramid; but they were not meant to be so obviously noticed. The upward and outward bevel on the underside of this boss does not aid the lifting boss theory either. Neither does the fact that it is noticeably offset to the west of the center of the semi-wall. Nor is there any evidence of a similar lifting boss on the larger, heavier lower section of the semi-wall. Even though the boss is remindful of the upper half of the split-beam of light, it is not correct in perspective, height or centering. However, the breadth of the face and the vertical distance from the bottom of the bevel to the height of the face are identical and equal to the Great Step valley bottom width of .2039840430 units (5 1/16 inches or 128.66 mm). So, the connection is there, but not as a direct geometric statement. Instead, it is a statement designed as a conjunction, symbolically using the reference beam to connect and emphasize the words "Hall of Light" and "light component parts." In a way, we see a somewhat similar symbolism in use today, usually for identifying dangers or hazards. Rather than written directions, a more commonly recognizable symbol is posted, such as for radiation exposure warning.

Having been diverted by this one small decoration within the Great Pyramid, we must return to the confirmation train of thought. We are at the lead edge of the first gate recess where the designer had finished his introductory Antechamber notation by redirecting our attention to the square root of e. Or, if you prefer, he made a transition back to continuing the "e" passage itself at the point of introducing the three symbolic movable gates. The thickness of each of these gates, or more properly the recess allowance for each symbolic gate, repeats the fingerprint word for the component parts of the speed of light. This triple redundancy statement is made for emphasis, pure and simple. By using this last phrase, pure and simple, you project white light by adding its three primary colors, or block it, by using the three primary color filters.

The movable gates were noted as symbolic or figurative for a couple of reasons. First and foremost is the difference in heights of the east and west passage side walls. The shorter east wall has a smooth shelf top, whereas the west wall has three semi-circular journal box depressions in its higher shelf top. These depressions would retain journals rotated to raise or lower the indicated gates, but the smooth top of the east wall would have allowed the journals to roll askew and become ineffective, unless an improbable, compound, east side drive mechanism were mounted on this shelf and left no evidence.

Not called to your attention during initiation was the second reason. To indicate three gates and to keep vertical movement aligned, two pairs of spaces were required the full gate travel distance. As a matter of fact, only the extreme top and foot of each is in place. Almost the entire theoretical operating range for gate retention is non-existent. To assume literal gates and vandalism overlooks the obvious: The hard rose granite spaces are missing far more central material than required to remove the gates themselves, but of even greater significance is that the stub top and foot portions are *uniformly* rounded and beveled into the extensive missing portion areas. More hard evidence can be cited to further substantiate symbolic gates, but our purpose is positive confirmation rather than becoming hung up on the truth of figurative gates.

Transition is indeed the lesson of the Antechamber. It is an interlude between the climactic message perceived at the Great Step and final confirmation thereof in the King's Chamber, or Confirmation Center. Certainly it adds to your fund of knowledge and a growing admiration for the designer. Within its limestone north wall, granite ceiling and the mixture of both in the floor and other three side walls, you have found the expansion of the word "light" to encompass both wavelength times frequency and three primary colors. A third subtle reference to the awe-inspiring genius of the designer and to the startling message of the Great Pyramid is found in the nature of the materials themselves. Limestone is a product of the sea, or by association, waves: Granite is granular, or by the same logic, associated with particles. Put the two concepts together and you have the contemporary theory for the nature of light, packets of pure energy (photons) moving in wave patterns.

The final portion of the "e" passage tells the initiate how to recognize that which he is seeking—confirmation. Just two known words are spoken here, e and four. No matter how clearly said, four times a natural function or logarithm, the truth is that the initiate will have momentary amnesia at the moment of truth. His reaction is normal for someone realizing the promise and the premise were correct and the truth self-evident. Trust does have to be earned, rather than given freely, to have value.

Confirmation proceeds directly upon entry into the King's Chamber. This first item on the agenda is the last of the multi-referenced mystery words, the width of this chamber north to south. I guided your review of the clues from entrance location to this final chamber. Yes, the number of minutes it takes for light to travel from the surface of the sun to the surface of the earth. Here is the redundancy reference to the minute measurement of time, which notation should have provoked you to open the question at the time of locating the entrance. The designer did subdivide the day into hours and minutes and by so doing pre-dated the current history regarding this subject. Perhaps the ancient Egyptians did not publish the fact that they had what was known as the "hour" watch early enough and let the credit go elsewhere.

The almost simultaneous discovery of the east-west length of the King's Chamber being two times the width is both a confirming repetition for emphasis and something else. As the width is a universal constant, ordained by the Creator, and a proof by application, by the logic of the noble relationship, the length says the speed of light and the sun-to-earth surfaces distance were known to mankind (the word two). Incidentally, if you stood at the mid-point of the north wall, you would be equidistant from each of the other three walls.

After this chamber's first dual proof of confirmation, the initiate begins to feel closer to the initial promise of the half-area level; point of message, expansion thereof, and now confirmation proof starting to turn into a warm, rosy glow. What is next? The last remaining chamber dimension, the height. This second King's Chamber proof turns out to be an interesting teaser, so the initiate knows it is not the final proof. The height of this Confirmation Center does confirm the words "four" and "ten," and both exponential and natural logarithm functions since it equals either $\ln 10^4$ or $\ln \sqrt[4]{10^{16}}$. You recall that 10^{16} times the word for light, 1.5, provides the designer's actual speed of light in Great Pyramid Units per solar year. Even more importantly, he makes this connection geometrically and with finality by having the envisioned extension of the Hall of Light floor line terminate at the chamber's south wall and ceiling juncture.

This finishing flourish of interior design leaves only the empty, open coffer holding the final confirmation. The fact that this single block of hewn, slightly more cocoa-colored granite sits astride the north-south central axis of the Great Pyramid reinforces this presumption because the speed of light message was discovered at the same half-area level but on the east-west central axis of the pyramid. This is the first clue of the coffer. The second clue is the volume of stone itself being found exactly equal to the volume of space enclosed. If this container were filled with water, as the designer suggests by his bathtub design, you find the proportional weight of the stone to the water to be exactly equivalent to e, for a third clue.

While we are discussing the coffer itself, which by now has become a source of amazingly accurate design information rather than merely an incomplete, standard, built-in tomb fixture, a couple of fascinating facets should be called to your attention. In thinking through to water content aspect, when it is used as a standard as noted for specific gravity, water is denoted as one, or unity. This brings us right back to the noble relationship usage denoting God. Yet today, the meaning of water is spiritual. The other facet of interest today is the *stone* container. If you divide its weight by 500, a British *stone* unit of weight measurement is found equal to 14 pounds avoirdupois. Coincidence or derivation, you make the choice, for the situation is similar to the case of the megalithic yard.

Regarding the coffer measurements, the puzzle is similar to that of the Niche. Remembering that the theme of the Great Pyramid message is built consistently around the word e, and that the coffer has very plainly just spoken this word, provides you with the clue to crack the coffer's design measurement code. This game is played until five points of significance allow resolution which turns out as variations on the theme of the natural logarithm of ten. That is, all goes well for the widths and heights, or four of the six dimensions. The fifth, inside length, is more troublesome but introduces common (Briggsian) logarithms to the base ten, but then points directly to the sixth dimension, outside length, as the key to final confirmation.

Here the designer plays his last card. With the ultimate in wit and teaching finesse he puts your confirmation in your hands. What is the password contained in the outside length dimension? You have been prepared: Will you be found worthy to be accepted into the fraternity of the enlightened? The momentary amnesia strikes: The question is asked again. Your mind begins to revive. Yes, it has become clear now, four times the outside dimensions equals the password, which is...just what the designer intended— that you convince yourself of the contention that mankind once knew with certainty the speed of light and all that may be inferred therefrom..."The natural logarithm of the speed of light."

Confirmation, yes; you said it yourself when you answered the third repeat of the question with the proper password itself. Humbled and thrilled that you have been found worthy of this honor, you hear the Great Pyramid give a sigh of relief and silently shout:

"So may it be."

XI. POSSIBILITIES AND PROBABILITIES

A word to the wise: Resolution of the mystery of design intent does bring to light a number of possibilities and probabilities, but does not of itself rule out existing explanations for the Great Pyramid, as we shall see. The two major contenders are based on the purpose of this edifice; namely, use for a tomb and use for prophecy. It is possible the Great Pyramid was so designed, placed and executed to fulfill a variety of purposes including knowledge transmittal, tomb and prophecy, but the probability of being all things to all people is extremely remote.

I started my work on understanding the Great Pyramid after hearing a lecture supporting the prophecy viewpoint. While it is true these supporters supply one of the best sources of relatively accurate dimensional facts, better than I have found for any other pyramid, I did not feel that close was good enough to count except in horseshoes and hand-grenades. As this research progressed and all close possibilities had to be ruled valid or extraneous, I found the prophecy theory did not precisely fit the design intent. Second, and more importantly, the prophecy school of thought tended to read the past in similar fashion, but varied widely in forecasting. A number of "end" dates have become history already. Thus, it would appear to be another case of "back to the drawing board" for prophecy. Prophecy does have popular appeal and still may be proven; however, its backers need to find a unified, supportable position or accept the self-inflicted appellation of false prophets.

If prophecy is to self-destruct, what then takes prominence for escape from the tomb school of thought? All in good time, for Khufu comes first. He has substantial evidence backing his claim with just a few of the touchstones being noted here:

— Chronologically, ancient accounts of kings of the various Egyptian dynasties place him at about the right place and time, IV Dynasty, Third Millenium, B.C.
— Prior pyramids indicate increasing sophistication of construction and later ones declining craftsmanship.
— Only a pharaoh could marshal the required resources.
— Pyramids were built as either actual tombs or tombs apparent.
— Adjacent constructions such as small attendant pyramids, funeral temple, causeway and boat pits fit the tomb thesis.
— At least one of the quarry marks found daubed on the blocks of the upper relieving chambers is a cartouche ascribed to Khufu.

Certainly, no other school of thought has undergone the scrutiny as a body of knowledge, nor bears the credentials of the pyramid as an intended tomb; or more exactly, as an intended repository for both mortal remains plus worldly possessions and as a home base for the soul or spirit of the deceased. Both the Ba (immortal soul) and the Ka (the genius or spiritual self) are keystones of ancient Egyptian religion. These attributes of man certainly set him apart from other creatures of the animal world and imply the existence of more than meets the eye. Just as this pyramid, the product of man's hand, is home for his immortal parts, why not also home for other eternal truths stemming from his intellect?

The Great Pyramid as a tomb certainly fits the known archeological facts, but these do not spell out why this particular design. Thus, this mathematical archeological discovery speaks for more noble and glorious purposes in addition to the apparent reasons for its existence. This encoding of timeless knowledge was so masterful in concept, design and execution, it becomes difficult to accept and believe the obvious. Yet, there it is with a solid set of clues or symbols saying, "Enshrined herein are living truths." Consider these things:

— The largest, most perfect, solid masonry structure ever crafted was contemporary to the Stone Age Neolithic period in western Europe about 10,000-2,500 B.C., and both the Sumerians and Babylonians are reputed to have advanced more in mathematics than the Egyptians of this period. However, it was in Egypt the true pyramid began to loom large.
— Strabo in 24 B.C. described a hinged stone, or flush flap door, on the north face of the Great Pyramid which was indistinguish-

able until raised for entry. Although possibly added as an alteration after completion, this is most improbable. One good reason being the sockets for a flap door found on the upper sides of the north face entrance to the south (Bent) pyramid of Sneferu at Dashur, which predates the Great Pyramid. So far, these two hinged stone doors are quite unique as the only reported cases of this type of closure.

— The passages and chambers of the Great Pyramid were designed with by far the greatest deviations from ground level of any Egyptian pyramid. This uniqueness has been inexplicable.

— The ventilation ducts, roughed in for the Queen's Chamber (Learning Center) and completed into the King's Chamber (Confirmation Center), are again unique to this Egyptian pyramid. However, some New World pyramids have ventilation ducts, but so far these found ventilate rooms seem to have been more likely used as preparatory spaces for ceremonial purposes.

— The Great Pyramid is more truly oriented to the cardinal directions, as we know them, than any other pyramid. This is a difficult feat, even today, when we realize true and magnetic north do not coincide and the latter also wanders.

Let there be no mistake! These points were designed. They are not coincidental nor accidental construction quirks. Neither were they required nor necessary for the established tomb purposes. Accepting the known facts of design then leads to the question of intent. Can a combination of uniqueness and precision, properly interpreted, disclose design intent? Absolutely! This is how most discoveries are tested and confirmed. The clues fit the facts; they are logical and sequential, and they lead to conclusions that can be substantiated by out present level of knowledge. Indeed, indicated greater precision, or depth of knowledge greater than our best, underscores our level, not that of the designer. Actually, what the Great Pyramid says is what he believed or knew, rather than what we would say from our current position in the scale of time and intellectual achievement. You cannot deny the fact, whether you can accept the implications or not, that the Great Pyramid can speak to you, and its message not only has seniority, but also commands respect.

By a wide margin, our acceptance of what is spoken to us by this pyramid is difficult due to our established patterns of thought. Not because it is illogical or without unique clues, but because of our egos. We prefer to believe we have progressed to our present level rather than returned partially to a former higher level of achievement, origin unknown. Thus, the question of independent evidence arises. My first response to this is to suppose our present civilization were destroyed and vandalized over the next 4500 years. What real evidence of our knowledge would survive? Very little, if any, although scattered remnants of our presence would tend to indicate we had been here. Without our libraries and knowledge systems, a few surviving epitaphs and inscriptions from public buildings would not place us very far up the intellectual ladder. Our documentation would be nil without maintenance.

However, there is another side to this cataclysmic scenario. We do have another side to our egos. This other side is curiosity to seek out our origins; to find supportive evidence for man's claim to dominance over the earth and a place in the universe. Mere chance or a standard result of the evolutionary process gives little comfort. Early evidence of intellectual achievement is much more substantial. Increasingly rapid progress in recent years is pushing both the origins and achievements of man ever further back in the span of time and providing the necessary time frame for the rise and decline of earlier civilizations.

So, what if the message of the Great Pyramid is startling? A surprise discovery often solves one mystery, then spawns others; a prize discovery clears the air a little more so that real truths may be established. This single step in mathematical archeology is a beginning, for maybe we have been neglecting the true value of our inheritance. Having jarred our complacent egos and aroused our inquiring egos by this discovery, the next step must be the testing of other pyramids by like methods, though not necessarily by the same standard of measurement. This will take some time since precise dimensions for other pyramids are scarce in available reference sources. To simplify such a sizable undertaking, the best bet will be to start with the Great Pyramid as a base time point and check both forward and backward in presumed sequence one by one. At the most, ten to either side (see Table 11-1) will quickly establish a pattern of answers to the following five key questions:

1. Is the Great Pyramid one of a kind, standing alone in tribute to the genius of one person?
2. If other pyramids are found to speak in similar terminology,

how does the trend fit the assumed chronology?
3. Can anything be learned to better focus on the full depth of the Great Pyramid message in a second or third interview?
4. Whence came this knowledge?
5. Where does this lead?

There are a number of fascinating aspects to answering these questions and far-reaching implications of so doing. The first question is not going to be the first answered, but it is the lead topic of inquiry. Actually, each of these queries may be sub-divided into further questions of procedures and questions of meanings. Or, if you like, how do we ask what, and how do we interpret the results? The message of the Great Pyramid is unique, no doubt about that; but beyond the spoken message is the vast grey area of who, what, why, when, where and how. With the discovery of the solution to the mystery of design intent, or why this particular design, the whole field of general interest commands even greater attention. So, also, do routine questions often lead to exciting possibilities and unexpected probabilities.

You see, the first key question is whether the Great Pyramid is unique. It does teach the message recipient how to conclude that the message is real without referring to sources other than known relationships. On your first interview, it does not tell you to go and listen to supplementary messages from other pyramids. In fact, it first tells you its unit of measurement of 24.8312 inches (630.714 mm), which is neither the ancient Egyptian sacred cubit of 25.026 inches (635.66 mm) nor royal cubit of 20.625 inches (523.86 mm). Neither is the Great Pyramid unit exactly equal to any other ancient system of measurement. It is possible we are seeing an aborted attempt by one person to set a standard unit of measurement based on the linear universal constant of the speed of light in a vacuum, but the probability is this would appear elsewhere, if so, carried on by a small number of informed initiates. Unless, of course, his transfer of knowledge were cut short for some reason. And this could be possible in that the basic design had been completed on the trestle board, but not all of the detailed drawings. Some evidence of this is found in the rough finish of the Learning Center floor, the same condition of the Transitional Chamber and the lessened construction quality above the Confirmation Center level.

Another point in this one-of-a-kind discovery is use of a logic sequence. The message builds up to a climax, then confirms, rather

Archaic Period: Dynasty III (2780-2680 B.C.)

Zoser	Saqqara	Step Pyramid
Sekhem-khet	Saqqara	Unfinished Step Pyramid
Kah-ba	Zawiet el Aryan	Layer Pyramid
Neb-ka	Zawiet el Aryan	Unfinished Pyramid
Hu (Huni)	Meydum	
? #1	Seila	
? #2	Zawiet el Aryan	
? #3	El Kola	

Old Kingdom: Dynasty IV (2680-2560 B.C.)

Sneferu	Dashur	S. Stone Pyramid (Bent)
Sneferu	Dashur	N. Stone Pyramid
Khufu	Giza	The Great Pyramid
Rededef	Abu Rawwash	
Khafre	Giza	The Second Pyramid
Menkure	Giza	The Third Pyramid

Old Kingdom: Dynasty V (2560-2420 B.C.)

Weserkaf	Saqqara	
Sahure	Abusir	
Neferirkare	Abusir	
Neferefre	Abusir	
Neuserre	Abusir	
Isesi	S. of Saqqara	
Wenis	Saqqara	

Table 11-1. King's Pyramids

than stating a specific number here and another there without regard to connecting links. This is most important to a convincing proof of design intent. Which is more convincing, an ordinary crossword puzzle or one designed to use each and every word to tell a complete, sensible story? It is much simpler to incorporate a few isolated pieces of information into a structure, but then they may be seen as coincidental, if discovered at all. The fact that many may wish the Great Pyramid would speak more directly, and in greater detail on a first encounter, completely misses the stupendous significance that it can be found to speak and be understood.

Addressing the second key question in light of the first, you see that a common unit of measurement cannot be assumed. This being so means other pyramids must be approached with the same method of mathematical archeology inquiry and an open mind. It is possible that none may speak in any dialect; all may, some may, or some may speak in a few word facts but without sentence structure. Depending on what is heard from these other potential witnesses, three distinct possibilities currently are vying in contention. The Great Pyramid design progressively evolved as a small cult of intellectuals developed and practiced integration of knowledge in design as royal commissions became available. Or, as a body of developed knowledge which had reached a zenith went into eclipse, the remaining practitioners decided to codify what they still could in commissioned stonework as total understanding ebbed away. Or, it could have been a one-shot deal, either in presumed sequence or as precursor model, with one designer or several, or with or without the assent of Khufu (or whoever commissioned its design). You can see how this possibility may turn into a can of worms or lead to the truth of the matter. Fantastic as it may seem at first glance, one or more pharaohs could have been fully initiated into the secrets-of-knowledge fraternity and deemed it prudent to use his resources to preserve a portion permanently in stone. What better way than to place it ostensibly as a tomb, or a tomb among tombs, even if he were to be placed in a far less obvious and therefore more secure resting place. You see, some pyramids do not appear to have been used for their obvious purpose; for example, why would Sneferu build two, both at Dashur, or Amenemhet III build two, one at Hawara and one at Dashur? It is necessary then to find if, what and how the other pyramids of this era speak to get a better fix on who, when, why, and maybe even how, the Great Pyramid acquired the gift of speech.

If the other pyramids can speak and be understood, the possibility exists that they may serve as tutors to focus on the full depth of the Great Pyramid message. The key question there is the "work smarter, not harder" approach to a second or third level interview. You have been initiated; now is anyone else around who can assist in preparing you for your next advancement, or by their silence attest to your traveling alone with the only authorized guide? There is so much more than this initial message. A second interview promises more insight into the applications of your initiation knowledge. Just two examples suggest a rich field of multi-variety information awaiting inquiry.

The first example is taken from the HP-35 Operating Manual. Although logarithms were originally used to speed multiplication and division, they have particular significance in scientific and engineering problems. There is, for example, a logarithmic relationship between altitude and barometric pressure. Suppose you wish to use an ordinary barometer as an altimeter. After measuring the sea level pressure (30 inches of mercury) you climb until the barometer indicates 9.4 inches of mercury. How high are you? Although the exact relationship of pressure and altitude is a function of many factors, a reasonable approximation is given by:

$$\text{Altitude (feet)} = 25{,}000 \ln \frac{30}{\text{Pressure}}$$

From the answer of 29,012 feet, you might suspect you may be on Mt. Everest (29,028 feet). Now, convert this into the Great Pyramid Unit of measurement. Use the reciprocal of the Learning Center ratio squared, or e divided by 2.25, which equals 1.208125257 (call it R for regular atmospheric pressure), and the relationship works out as:

$$\text{Altitude (Units)} = (R \times 10^4)\left(\ln \frac{R}{\text{Pressure}}\right)$$

$$= (R \times 10^4)\left(\ln \frac{R}{.378556}\right)$$

$$= 14{,}020 \text{ Units } (29{,}011 \text{ feet})$$

The second example is lunar, rather than terrestrial, but again uses the same R value as just calculated above. The orbit of the moon is much more difficult to define than the orbit of the earth. One of the moon orbit variables is called the 18.61-year lunar cycle. Its rising and setting points furthest north and south gradually move inward from the extremes until mid-cycle; then they back away again to the extremes. These two turning points, or standstills, each allow a brief period of several days in which a smaller orbital variable may be observed. This very small perturbation (wobble) has a cycle of 173.3 days and is significant in that eclipses can occur only when it is near maximum. Therefore, having an important reason for noting the lunar cyle and a compatible medium for ready reference resulted in recording the relationship as:

$$\text{Lunar Cycle (years)} = \ln(R \times 10^8) = 18.60975$$

As you can see, it is well worth the effort to check other pyramids for advice on more quickly comprehending not only what is included in the Great Pyramid message, but how. Again, no help may be found, and we will be back to the only expert witness with a multitude of relationships to disclose, and interrelationships to expose, in a second interview. Why a thorough understanding of this step is so important comes with the realization that a third interview promises further insight into application of the second step. The third level is designed to teach that which is unknown and therefore not presently recognizable. These secrets we would like to know, such as anti-gravity or control of other forms of energy, can provide vast benefits to mankind and also explain more of "how" such mediums were actually brought into being.

Such perception naturally leads to the fourth key question of whence came this knowledge. In general, there are only a handful of potential sources which are in contention for more specific investigation. This knowledge had to come from one of these five sources:

Local Egyptian development and organization.

Imported from another contemporary civilization.

Imported from a lost civilization.

Imported from an extra-terrestrial civilization.

Imported by an act of divine guidance.

In effect, each of these is a little further out. But, even as probability diminished, if you believe possession is nine tenths of the law, then the Egyptians have it hands down. However, the source question is still open. Even if this is a home-grown product, was outside assistance involved? For example, the quarry marks found dabbed on the hidden faces of some of the stone blocks have reported incidences of wrong facing glyphs, such as a child printing ƆAT for cat. Does this infer a semi-literate quarry foreman (or project coordinator) or allow for the possibility of someone on their lunch hour teaching a local worker to write in hieroglyphics? What about the reverse, an Egyptian teaching an outsider the local written language? The point here is the Great Pyramid speaks of precise advanced knowledge for which present reference sources do not give the ancient Egyptians of the pyramid era credit. Even calling it Hermetic arcanum, or secret mystery, previously unproven, leaves the question of source wide-open.

If indeed the ancient Egyptians did have problems using and expressing fractions, much less more advanced mathematical concepts, what about their contemporaries? Could the required information have been imported by a secret cult devoted to knowledge? There are glimmers of scattered advanced Stone Age knowledge all around the world, but no concentrated source identified. So, unless the Egyptians were world-wide travelers and importers of information and technology, which is not recognized, a contemporary civilization source seems highly unlikely. Nearby civilizations do not show the great difference in potential required to produce the giant intellectual leap exhibited by the Great Pyramid.

The next potential source, a lost civilization, offers intriguing possibilities and some fair probabilities, then leaves the whence-came-this-knowledge question unanswered but removed one step backward. Assume, for example, an advanced civilization were concentrated in a particular geographic area, and through natural or self-induced catastrophe very suddenly met oblivion. If a small scattered number of inhabitants had been absent or survived the big event, wherever they went stories of what had been would be told to the primitive peoples in exchange for survival assistance. In this way a common unit of measurement, such as the megalithic yard, could have appeared in widely scattered general use. If only one or two of these expatriates carried the advanced knowledge, rather than just knowing of its existence or results, they would have a tremendous impact on a receptive, nubile culture. By whatever title, be it vizier, priest, medicine man, shaman or innumerable others, the effective exile was positioned to perpetuate some of what had been known. The legends that abound in every culture about visits of wise men, or their return, or of lost civilizations may very well have had a basis in fact. Atlantis or Lemuria could conceivably have seeded the knowledge that grew into the design of the Great Pyramid.

If this is speculative, as the word oblivion denotes, even more speculative is knowledge imported from an extra-terrestrial source. This could be direct as a UFO encounter in ancient Egypt, or indirect as an extra-terrestrial colony becoming a lost civilization. The latter would seem more probable in light of the use of the universal constant, the speed of light, being expressed in terrestrial measurement. That is, the exact length of the solar year is peculiar to, and only to, the earth. Would man in an encounter with a primitive civilization of another world be as intelligent in promoting a system of measurement in their world-related units or would our exploratory crew try to impose our ways upon them? On a visit, I doubt we would make the effort to precisely determine units of best fit for their use, whereas as permanent colonizers, we would be more inclined to adapt to their particular conditions: Most inclined if return were impossible or inconceivable.

The fifth and last of the whence-came possibilities is divine guidance. Here again this could have been direct or indirect assistance. Direct as in the case of access to the mind of the designer by dream inspiration (prophecy), or indirect as in the case of the materialization as a human form of the Supreme Architect of the Universe (incarnation). However improbable, these divine possibilities exist because they cannot be ruled out per se on the basis of present evidence. One special case must be noted that in effect could tie divine guidance with one or more of the other four possible sources: Imhotep. It seems he was one of those universal geniuses renowned as sage, scribe, architect, vizier, chief ritualist, doctor and magician who was a minister of the pharaoh Zoser of the third dynasty (about 2780 B.C.). This remarkable man was later deified in the 26th dynasty, or Saite period, c. 664-525 B.C. Could he have designed or taught the principles later incorporated in the Great Pyramid? It is possible, and also possible that Imhotep did belatedly receive recognition of his true status and stature. However, even though Imhotep is credited with first designing completely in stone, the first true pyramid came a century later according to our best information, which may not be completely accurate.

Although the source of the Great Pyramid knowledge has yet to be traced, the fact of its existence is amazing. Someone in ancient history knew the speed of light. The significance of this extends far beyond this simple statement itself. Today, we are still trying for an accurate measurement of this constant. But there is much more to this constant than just knowing its magnitude; it is useful in a variety of applications. Thus, if the designer knew Einstein's now famous formula, $E = mc^2$, the key to atomic energy, he really only had to speak of c in precise terminology to get his message across. Certainly, this is a message by inference, yet there is purported evidence of ancient atomic explosions such as one listed in India dated about 2400 B.C. Did someone learn from the message of the Great Pyramid two centuries after it had been constructed and go home to experiment? To digress on this topic of atomic energy for a moment, even though it is not part of the initial interview, what further evidence may the Great Pyramid suggest? Can you imagine the apprentice to the brotherhood of knowledge on his second interview passage entering the Confirmation Center and having the gates close behind him? In utter darkness, he would be asked to approach the coffer and when close upon it, he would find it filled with water as predicted in his initiation. But to his astonishment he can see light from within: A pale blue-green light from deep within the water which turns to blackness against the rose granite of the chamber. Is it possible he is seeing an early atomic pile causing the water around it to glow? It could be so if certain clues can be made to speak. For example, what about the slight discoloration of the coffer—irradiation induced? What about residual radiation levels—any higher than would be expected, or can we not yet measure that finely? What about the gates themselves, if actually in place—figurative filters, but literal movable shieldings? What about the boss—an offset relief symbol for the beam of light behind in the Hall of Light and symbolic warning of radiation hazard ahead and to the west? And what about the coffer itself—was the ratio of stone to that of the heavy water on the cut-down upper rear edge (usually assumed to be for a missing sliding lid) really equivalent to the water volume reduction required for the equivalent weight of heavy water? And what about the fact that earlier mummies are better preserved—was the additional step of preservation by irradiation originally practiced during the traditional seventy-day mummification period? As you can see, the entered apprentice has yet far to travel in his quest for more light. Ponder these things as you go forth: Irradiated diamonds change color, irradiated foods are preserved, pyramids and pyramid shapes appear to arrest decay, the ventilation shafts in the King's Chamber may have been designed for more reasons that those previously listed; in a search of the second pyramid of Giza (Khafre) for hidden interior cavities the scintillation counter readings did not correlate; and, if you will, the plaque at the University of Chicago dedicated to Enrico Fermi and Pile 1 under the west stands of Stagg Field, which reads:

On December 2, 1942
Man Achieved Here
The First Self-Sustaining Chain Reaction

And Thereby Initiated the
Controlled Release of Nuclear Energy.

To return to application examples for the speed of light, another example is the use of this constant for physical and astronomical measurements leading to precise knowledge of not only the solar system but also the universe. As stated by the total length of the sloped passages, distances could be accurately known along with calculations of sizes, masses, gravitational constants and so on. The point here is, if much is known but the medium of communication is limited, speak first in a recognizable idiom denoting the level of achievement you wish the recipient to perceive. However, let us not take our level to have been the same as that of the designer of the Great Pyramid. After all, he was smart enough to speak to us late-comers. We still generally think of the speed of light (in a vacuum) as an absolute constant of nature, which when approached, causes strange effects on our perception of time and mass. It is mathematically possible to have a consistent universe on the other side of the speed of light. This means we have yet to break the "light barrier." And when we do, we could find our ancestors had been there too.

Before we forget where we are, a look at the fifth and final key question is in order: Where does this lead? The obvious direction is the Great Pyramid statement, "Look to a star at 311.4883214 light-years distance from the earth." Why? Besides proving knowledge of precise astronomic measurement and pinpointing with certainty the stellar dating of the message, did the indicated knowledge possibly come from there? Is that how such a precise measurement of the distance became known? Is this the address of our nearest neighbors of relatives? Or is this a clue to our next move in a gigantic game of treasure hunt? Whatever this direction represents, it calls for action to find out where it does lead. This may be easier said than proven as more than one party may reside at the same address. But given directions to the correct neighborhood is a start for the quest. The real problem may be changes in the neighborhood, or residence, due to elapsed time. What we are looking for may be out of existence by now, but we will never know if we do not follow up on the direction given. So far, this is the best direction we have been given. Unfortunately, our best in distance measurement and communication may be none too good for the task. With improvement in these areas, however, we can find if there is further significance to this specific star distance. Here again, the Great Pyramid speaks to you, for each of us would like to know where this does lead. It is our guide and counselor.

In all probability, the Great Pyramid will change what we believe true today. It would appear that as knowledge and control over energy declined, political power and control over material things took their place: The ends replaced the means in importance. Denial of a prior high-water mark is easy, but changing beliefs can be most difficult. Often progress comes from openly reviewing what is commonly accepted and taken for granted. For example, a cartouche is described as a royal name or identification consisting of several glyphs surrounded by an oval. No inscribed cartouches are found in or on the Great Pyramid. Yet on the basis of hidden daubed quarry marks showing a number of differing cartouches, one was identified as like or similar to one for Khufu. Somewhat worrisome, however, is the fact that reference sources vary in specific identification of which one it was and in what context it was used. We could be seeing a "Kilroy was here" situation. Was he? And if so, Kilroy who?

Also of interest are the reputed effects of aging. Even the earliest descriptions and sketches show the wear and tear attributed to countless visitors. This could be so, even though for centuries at a time, no one set foot in this temple or tomb. But, on closer examination of this expert witness, we find why it is necessary to interrogate other potential witnesses as to what has been spoken to us. The most abraded surfaces are the ones most critical to the correct message interpretation. Why? First, of course, is the use of the floors as the solid basis for message storage and transmittal. But other critical edges and surfaces appear to have been deliberately defaced by persons unknown who knew where the least damage would be most effective. We could be seeing a situation of someone deciding the encoded knowledge was becoming too dangerous for mankind to have: a case of silencing a witness who cannot be eliminated.

One feature which could not be eliminated deserves more attention: namely, the vents. Which of the senses did these represent? Here more detailed facts plus research insight and perception are required. The Confirmation Center vents may have a connection with sound, either hearing or production, for they have peculiarly shaped enlargements, like resonating chambers, situated at the base of what could be open organ pipes. On the other hand, if the south vent is straight (unlike the investigated north vent), it would twice a year allow the sun to shine directly down its bore to the horizontal enlarged section. We could be seeing the designer using the redundancy principle again as a multi-purpose feature. The eventual answer will be found when hard facts can be matched to thinking as he thought.

One other aspect of design begging for comment is, why did the designer choose the word 1.5 to represent the speed of light? Why not base a standard system of measurement on a unity origin; that is, 1×10^{16} as a basis? This would have provided a basic unit of 37 1/4 inches or 946.07 mm, which would be somewhat more than a three-foot yard and somewhat less than a meter. However, since the people of that era were shorter than today's average, the Great Pyramid unit would more fairly represent one pace to them. Another practical aspect is that the word 1.5 was available and readily recognizable by the recipient. But most likely is the noble relationship basis of "one" for God and "two" for mankind with light, or enlightenment, spanning the distance between them and represented verbally by the midpoint word. Or if you prefer, let God represent pure energy (E) and mankind matter (m), then the speed of light would be the connecting constant (c) to the power of the understanding of man (2).

While we are discussing the spiritual nature of the designer, not his religious convictions, a quick look forward along the path of history can help verify the status of his enlightenment. Research indicates good probability that Moses was an initiate of the Great Pyramid. After freeing his people from their bondage in Egypt, he charges them with the obligation that they shall not hate an Egyptian, for they were visitors in the land of Egypt (Deut. 23:7) This obligation sounds strange except in light of payment for knowledge received. Confirmation of this speculation is found in the New Testament (Acts 7:22), which states without reservation that Moses learned all Egyptian wisdom: "And Moses was instructed in all the wisdom of the Egyptians; and he was mighty in his words and works." Further along the path of history is the contention that Jesus Christ was also an initiate during the unrecorded years between his confirmation and ministry. As an initiate, consider the company you may be keeping.

The recital of possibilities and probabilities could go on almost endlessly and become ever more speculative. This is not the intent nor should it be the goal. The purpose must be to provide direction for inquiry with the objective of finding the truth. It is true that direct access to desired information is limited, but this does not stop discovery of information. We can regret that so much of value has been lost or destroyed. Or worse yet, become narrow-minded and oblivious to everything outside of our pet prejudices. How much more exciting is the thrill of the hunt and serendipity of discovery. Just suppose, in light of the Great Pyramid speaking, some of the existing records of the past were to be looked at again with fresh eyes. I do not believe for one minute that we truly understand all there is to know in what has been found or will be found. Wherever possible, attention must be focused on original source information since subsequent alterations or interpretations tend to introduce error. Other sources have tended to be overlooked or explored from only one point of view. One of these may be the ancient archives of the Coptic Church. These original Egyptian Christian records apparently escaped much of the suppression of information inflicted upon so many firsthand sources. I mention this because two interpretations of the roots of the word pyramid are light measurement (or fire in the middle) and count by tens (or decimalization). The etymology of the former is Grecianized Semitic and the latter is Coptic.

Attention! This is the silent shout of the Great Pyramid of Giza. Since it calls for attention, your attention, how should it be approached? Simply with an open mind, if it is to speak to you of interesting and wondrous things. To impart knowledge requires both an intelligible speaker and a receptive petitioner. Of the latter, some may choose to disbelieve even one hundred percent proof of mathematical archeology; some may choose to mentally file the message to await further developments; and some may choose to not only accept initiation, but also to look forward to more and further enlightenment. You have approached of your own free will; so, what of the message will you carry with you?

First, the exact configuration of the Great Pyramid may be fully accounted for: Design intent is proven.

Second, the knowledge and presentation are of a higher level than our contemporary civilization has produced: Awe-inspiring genius is proven.

Third, the implications of the message are startling, for it tells us our ancestors had traveled this way before. Positive identification of the source has yet to be made.

We have solved one mystery, why the Great Pyramid calls for your attention, with a clue-by-clue revelation of an unsuspected message. It is not obvious "who dunnit", or why, but we are now obligated to continue to follow, then, the rest of the mystery, as if it were obvious. As you have discovered, those with open ears can hear the Great Pyramid speak, and regardless of how the message is accepted, you can never forget that The Great Pyramid Speaks To You of light, of life, of learning and of Love.

The End

BIBLIOGRAPHY

Badawy, Alexander. "A History of Egyptian Architecture." Vol. I. Giza: The Studio Misr in Giza, Egypt, 1954.

Benavides, Rodolfo. "Dramatic Prophecies of the Great Pyramid." Mexico City: Editores Mexicanos Unidos, S.A., 1970.

Breasted, James Henry. "A History of Egypt." New York: Charles Scribner's Sons, 1909.

Breasted, James Henry. "Ancient Records of Egypt." 5 Vols. Chicago: University of Chicago Press, 1906-07.

Brunton, Paul. "A Search in Secret Egypt." New York: Samuel Weiser, 1973.

Budge, E.A. Wallis. "The Egyptian Book of the Dead." New York: Dover Publications, Inc., 1967.

Capt, E. Raymond. "The Great Pyramid Decoded." Thousand Oaks, Calif.: Artisan Sales, 1971.

Davidson, David. "The Great Pyramid." London: Williams & Norgate, 1927.

Davidson, David. "The Great Pyramid, Its Divine Message." London: Williams & Norgate, 1932.

Edgar, John and Morton. "The Great Pyramid Passages and Chambers." London: Elliot Stock, 1910.

Edwards, I.E.S. "The Pyramids of Egypt." Baltimore, Md: Penguin Books, Inc., 1961.

Erman, Adolf. "Life in Ancient Egypt." New York: Dover Publications, Inc., 1971.

Fakhry, Ahmed. "The Pyramids." Chicago: University of Chicago Press, 1974.

Flanagan, G. Pat. "Pyramid Power." Glendale, Calif.: Pyramid Publishers, 1973.

Grant, Joan. "Winged Pharaoh." New York: Berkley Medallion Books, 1969.

Hall, Manley Palmer. "The Secret Teachings of All Ages." Los Angeles: Philosophical Research Society, Inc., 1972.

Hawkins, Gerald S. "Stonehenge Decoded." New York: Dell Publishing Co., Inc., 1965.

Hitching, Francis. "Earth Magic." New York: William Morrow and Co., Inc., 1977.

Hynek, J. Allen and Vallee, Jacques. "The Edge of Reality." Chicago: Henry Regnery Co., 1975.

Jenkins, Louise F. "General Catalogue of Trigonometric Stellar Parallaxes." New Haven, Conn.: Yale University Press, 1963.

Lauer, Jean Philippe. "Le Probleme Des Pyramides D'Egypte." Paris: Payot, 1948.

Lauer, Jean Philippe. "Le Mystere Des Pyramides." Paris: Presses de la Cite, 1974.

Lehner, Mark. "The Egyptian Heritage." Virginia Beach, Va.: A.R.E. Press, 1974.

Lemesurier, Peter. "The Great Pyramid Decoded." New York: St. Martin's Press, 1977.

Mendelssohn, Kurt. "The Riddle of the Pyramids." New York: Praeger Publishers, 1974.

Moore, Patrick. "A Guide to the Stars." New York: W.W. Norton Co., Inc., 1960.

Petrie, W.M. Flinders. "The Pyramids and Temples of Gizeh." London: Field & Tuer, The Leadenhall Press, 1885.

Schul, Bill and Pettit, Ed. "The Secret Power of Pyramids." Greenwich, Conn.: Fawcett Publications, Inc., 1975.

Scott, Joseph and Lenore. "Egyptian Hieroglyphs for Everyone." New York: Funk & Wagnalls, 1968.

Seiss, Joseph A. "The Great Pyramid: A Miracle in Stone." Blauvelt, N.Y.: Rudolf Steiner Publications, 1973.

Smith, Warren. "The Secret Forces of the Pyramids." New York: Kensington Publishing Corp., 1976.

Tompkins, Peter. "Secrets of the Great Pyramid." New York: Harper & Row, 1971.

Toth, Max and Nielsen, Greg. "Pyramid Power." New York: Freeway Press, Inc., 1974.

INDEX

A

Abusir 109, 125
Accuracy 20, 22, 27, 31, 40, 90, 113, 118, 120
Age (see Dating)
Aggregate 36, 104
Air, pressure 43, 57, 127
Akhnaton 105
Almighty (see God)
Alphabet 38, 43, 50
alpha,
 Cygni 81, 82
 Draconis 46, 81, 82, 107, 112
 Lyrae 81, 82
 Ursae Minoris 46, 81, 82, 107
Alteration 122
Altitude 57, 127
Amenemhet III 126
Amenhotep IV (see Chuen'eten)
Ancient,
 civilizations 65, 78, 97, 110, 112, 117, 120-122, 135
 units of measurement 25, 26, 36, 109-110, 112, 124-126, 129-130
Angle (see Slope)
Antechamber 37, 83-89, 113, 116-117

Anti-gravity 128
Apex 29, 32, 46, 47, 71
Aphelion 106-107
Arab 71
Arcanum 34, 128
Archeology 121-122, 123, 126, 135
Architect 97, 110, 130
Architecture 21, 22
Archives 135
Area 32, 71-72
Art (see Decoration)
Ascending (see Passages)
Assumption 26, 33, 35, 36, 102
Astronomical, measurement 81, 82, 112, 132
Astronomy 81, 82, 112
Atlantis 129
Atmosphere 127
Atomic 130-132
Autumn 27
Axis,
 passage 80, 81, 111-112
 pyramid 80, 94, 111-112, 117

B

Ba 121
Babylonian 121

139